FROM
RANCH
TO
Royalty

FROM
RANCH
TO
Royalty

*Memoirs of a Northern California
Cattleman's Daughter*

The Autobiography of
Pat Simson Arnold

XULON PRESS

Xulon Press
2301 Lucien Way #415
Maitland, FL 32751
407.339.4217
www.xulonpress.com

ISBN-13: 978-1-6628-1878-3

Table of Contents

Introduction

To everything there is a season.
A time to every purpose under the heaven.
A time to be born and a time to die.
— Ecclesiastes 3:1

I was born in Surprise Valley in Modoc County, California, in February 1932. It was named Surprise Valley by early immigrants heading west via wagon trains out of the Nevada territory. When they suddenly stumbled upon about fifty miles of poplar trees, streams, grassy meadows, alkali lakes, and luxuriant fields of clover and wild rye, they called the valley what it was: a lovely surprise. The prime year of settlement was 1804.

I am writing this book for a few different reasons. One is to show you what it was like growing up on a ranch in California in the early 1900s. We were still using teams of horses to do our haying and work up the fields for planting. I rode my horse, Pepper, to school nearly two miles away in town. Once we made it to town, we would stop at a barn my uncle and aunt kept their milk cows in. (Everyone had a cow because there was no milk in the stores in those days.) After my trek to the school from the ranch, I would stable Pepper in their barn and put hay out for him before crossing the street to the schoolhouse, carrying my books in a pillowcase.

As a child of a rancher, I was herding cattle by the time I was five. My childhood memories involve horses, cattle, sheep, fishing, hunting, and the rich earth of Northern California. It was a different time and a different way of living. In this memoir, I want to give you a glimpse of daily life during that era.

But I also have a spiritual purpose for writing this book. I can see how God has protected my family and moved in my life, and I want to share those memories with you. The story begins years before I was born, when God spared my father's life.

My dad was born in 1896. When he was about fourteen years old, he lived in Eagleville, which is seventeen miles south of Cedarville, the community where I grew up. Every child started working at a young age back then. You always work when you grow up on a ranch.

One cold day in February 1911, my dad, Bert, started getting supplies ready on horseback, to take up to a sheep camp located in Little High Rock Canyon across the California-Nevada border. Before he left, one of the ranchers who lived nearby told him, "Bert, I'll go ahead and take the supplies." So my dad stayed in Eagleville.

The rancher never returned. After several days, a search party was sent out to locate him. When they arrived at the sheep camp, they found the rancher and three other sheepherders murdered. A renegade Native American named Shoshone Mike and a band of other marauders from the Duck Valley reservation had attacked the camp, stolen the sheep, and massacred everyone they found.

When word got back to Surprise Valley about the massacre, the authorities formed a posse to search for the band of roving Shoshones. They spent several weeks tracking them in freezing winter weather. The massive manhunt finally ended in a shootout. Four members of the band survived—Shoshone Mike's three younger siblings and his daughter

By volunteering to take those supplies, that rancher saved my dad's life. I can see how God divinely intervened to protect the destiny He had for my father's family—for me, my children, and my children's children. God knows the plans He has for us. They are plans for good and not for evil, to give us a future and a hope (Jeremiah 29:11).

This book is a collection of stories I remember from my past. I hope it makes you laugh and that it blesses and encourages you. As you read it, maybe you will be able to see more clearly how the hand of God has moved in your own life.

The possemen who apprehended Shoshone Mike after the Little High Rock Canyon Massacre.

The Devil or His Grandmother!

*R*ight off the bat, I lived up to my Surprise Valley heritage. My parents were hard-working ranchers who thought they had finished having children eight years earlier when my sister, Jean, was born. My mother was around forty years old when I was unexpectedly conceived.

The doctor told her, "Barbara, if you don't want this baby, all I have to do is put the IUD back in, and you would just automatically pass it on." But my mother wasn't interested in that option. My parents wanted to keep me.

Surprise Valley didn't get a lot of snow, but the wind could be fierce in the winter, and it would blow the snow into deep drifts, making the roads nearly impassable. As my mother's time drew near, the doctor told her, "You can't have the baby at your house. Your husband needs to move you somewhere else before it snows and the lane drifts so full of snow that I can't get to you."

My cousin was married to the doctor's son, so my mother moved in with them during the last month of her pregnancy. I was born on February 7, in the middle of winter. Of course I had no choice in that.

I had a wonderful childhood. I was the youngest and was treated with love, but my siblings generally considered me a nuisance because of the age gap.

1

When I was born, Earl, my oldest brother, was fourteen years old and in high school. Bud was eleven and Jean was eight, so as the youngest, I was often in the way. I remember wandering down to the barn while my brothers were milking cows by hand, and they would squirt milk at me and the barn cat that would sit beside me, hoping for similar treatment. My brothers would drench me with raw milk. To this day, I rarely drink milk! There is something about the smell.

One day when I was four, Bud hopped on his bike and went to get the mail at the post office two miles down the road in town. The lane to the main road was rocky and graveled. I wanted to go with him, but I wasn't fast enough on my little tricycle. I followed him for a while, but he kept getting farther and farther ahead of me.

It was getting to be late in the day. The sun had set, and it was starting to get dark. I often went barefoot in the summer months, and as the shadows lengthened, I stopped on the road to strip off my shoes. I tied them to the handlebars of my tricycle and decided that since my brother hadn't waited for me, I would turn around and head home.

My dad had erected a split-log-and-barbwire fence around our property. As I rode past the fence, which was a little distance from the road, I suddenly saw movement. Something was over there—on the other side of the post. In the gathering dark, I could see what looked like a woman's hair. I was so frightened that my heart leapt in my chest, and I slammed my feet on the pedals to get away.

When I got home, breathless and scared, my dad was sitting in his chair reading the newspaper. He could see I was upset and asked what had happened.

Wide-eyed, I told him, "Well, I either saw the devil or his grandmother!"

Later, I found out the movement by the fence posts had been *my* mother. She had been following me the whole time, going from fence post to fence post, trying to conceal herself while keeping an eye on me. My words that night became a family joke that was repeated for years. Whenever the family got together, they would tell the story of the time I saw the "devil or his grandmother!"

Patsy and her tricycle.

The Horse that Went Loco

When I was about four years old, my dad bought me my first horse. I named him Bill. (I later married a man named Bill, so I guess you could say this name has always fascinated me.) He was an old black-and-white pinto, perfect for a child just learning how to ride. I was small enough that I had to stand on a manger to climb up onto the saddle.

One day, I had the clever idea that I would use a different type of bridle on Bill, one typically used on a much younger horse. It's called a snaffle bit and is milder than the one I typically used, designed for a horse that is not yet accustomed to a heavier bridle, as younger horses' mouths are softer, and the reins were not attached to each other.

I put the split-rein bridle on Bill and thought it looked lovely. I was so proud that I was using it—I was really something! Bill and I cantered up my parents' long driveway on our way into town to get the mail.

As we passed a neighbor's house on the way home, one of their dogs raced out and started barking at us. Bill jumped violently—and I lost the reins because they weren't tied together. They fell to the ground, and I was too small to reach forward and grab them as they hung off the bridle. Bill took off at a crazed gallop. There was nothing I could do except hold on to the saddle horn. For two miles, I cried, prayed, and screamed.

My dad had shipped hogs to market that day, and he'd left both corral gates open. As Bill and I tore across the ranch, we ran through both gates into the corral and down into a feedlot where our dairy cows would go after being milked to lie down. The field along the creek was gravelly, with five-foot willow bushes that hid the milk cows as they lay chewing their cud.

My dad was working in the corral, and as I zipped passed him he realized I was completely terrified on a runaway horse, and took off after us.

Bill, running as fast as he could through the willows and blinded with fright, ran right into the cows lying on the other side of the bushes. He fell on top of them, throwing me off his back. I was screaming and crying. I was really hysterical. I couldn't stand up. When I tried, I just kept falling because my legs and body were shaking due to the wild ride I had just endured.

When my dad finally reached me, he thought my leg was broken. He kept asking, "Is your leg broke?"

"No," I cried. "It's okay."

He picked me up and carried me back to the house because I was still so scared.

As it turned out, I didn't get a spanking for using the snaffle bit on an old horse. The first lesson to learn on a ranch: Use the right riding equipment.

Patsy on Bill. Brother Bud on Sandy. All ready for the Modoc County Fair Parade, 1936.

The Swallow Egg Meal

*B*efore Surprise Valley had electricity, Dad bought us a generator. He put it in an underground cellar, and to create more space for it, he built a new area into a combination woodshed, cellar, and washroom.

To insulate the cellar, my dad put shredded redwood bark between the walls, which helped the cellar stay about forty degrees year round. He had a butcher block he would use to cut up beef or lamb, just as they would in a butcher shop, and then he'd hang the meat up on hooks attached to a board running from one side of the cellar wall to the other. The meat would hang for a week or two to cure and tenderize it, which preserved it and made it taste much better. Whenever Mother decided the menu for the day, be it steak, a roast, or a tougher cut to be boiled, Dad would take the side down off the hook and cut off whatever amount we needed. We also had a meat grinder to turn tough meat into hamburger.

Along one side of the butcher block were several pickling barrels or crocks. Despite the name, these weren't used just to make pickles from our cucumbers, but also to cure hams and other foods. She would shred cabbage to go into a crock to cure with salt brine for sauerkraut.

We stored carrots we had grown in our large garden, and they would keep for several months. On the north end of the cellar, I remember shelves where she put her canned fruits and vegetables. Our orchard produced a good number of apples each year. We didn't have a cider press to make cider or vinegar, but I remember my dad and I would box up many of the windfall apples and take them up to a neighbor who had a press. After pressing, we would pour the cider into five-gallon cans, carry them home, and pour them into one-gallon jugs, which we kept in the cellar.

On the other end of the building was the washroom, which housed my mother's wringer washing machine. Every Monday, she would heat big tubs of water on the trash burner stove and wash our clothes, hanging them to dry on the line out in the yard. The trash burner stove was small but large enough to hold a metal washtub or, as I discovered, a little frying pan.

Since I was the youngest of four children and pretty much raised like an only child, I had to make up ways to entertain myself. By the time I was ten, two of my siblings had already married. The exception was my brother Earl, who was in the Air Force. Most of the time, I played around the barns and sheds located on our home ranch.

Every year during the summer months, swallows would build mud nests in the corral buildings so they could lay their eggs and hatch their young. One day I had an idea: I should make my own breakfast. I could knock down a mud swallow nest and get the eggs. They would have to be fresh eggs, of course, with no little swallows in them. But swallow eggs weren't enough—I wanted a full meal: eggs, bacon, and toast! I would need a frying pan to fry up the bacon, too. I asked Mother if she could make me a fire in the washroom, and I told her my idea. I was pretty excited about it.

Amazingly, Mother went along with my plan and cut off a few pieces of bacon from the slab we had hanging in our cellar. I went down to a shed located in the large corral next to the creek that ran through our property. I took along a big stick so I could knock down some nests, and I managed to dig out of the rubble several eggs that hadn't broken in the fall.

I returned to the washroom to make my great swallow egg meal. In the end, when everything was finally cooked and eaten, it wasn't as wonderful as I thought it would be—but what can you expect from an eight-year-old trying to entertain herself?

Patsy & friend saddled up and ready to ride.

No Bark and All Bite

$\mathcal{W}$hen I was about five years old, my folks went to Reno and bought a bunch of new furniture. My sister, Jean, and I received new twin beds made of maple, and I was pretty impressed with them. I wanted to sleep in mine *and* in Jean's, but she wouldn't let me.

She and I shared a bedroom that had a door onto a screened porch. Jean insisted on sleeping in the bed by the porch door. That was *her* bed, and I was not allowed to be in it.

At about 4,500 feet in elevation, Cedarville would get those crazy summertime thunderstorms with lots of lightning. Jean never liked them, but they didn't bother me. One particular night, there was a ferocious thunderstorm. Lightning lit up the sky and, as the thunder rolled and crashed, Jean shot out of bed and woke me up.

"Pat! Change beds with me!" she cried.

I had been sound asleep. The storm wasn't bothering me a bit. Any other time, the bed by the door was hers, but during a storm, all bets were off.

The next day, I told my mother, "I'm tired of Jean not ever letting me sleep in that bed except when there's a thunderstorm going with lightning, and she is afraid and wakes me up. Will you tell her to let me sleep in that bed?"

So Mother did and, for a while, Jean let me sleep there.

One day, my mother and sister were washing dishes. I was standing beside the woodstove, and I must not have been very old at the time, because I was about even with the stovetop. The window right above the sink looked out over a meadow where a big poplar tree stood.

Suddenly, lightning struck that poplar tree and almost split it in half. My sister screamed as chunks of the tree shot across the meadow. We didn't find too many pieces in our yard, but my dad found a big piece way down at the very end of our property, hundreds of feet from the strike.

We went to check out the shattered tree, of course, right after it happened. It was pretty damp on the inside because it was standing in the meadow where a lot of water was. I don't know if the moisture was the reason, but much of the tree wasn't charred. The bark had been blown away, and the wood in the center was sizzling. That's one of the main things I remember—I could hear the tree. It was making noises. You could see steam coming out of it and could actually *smell* smoke and the ozone from the electrical charge. It was pretty interesting.

Remarkably, the lightning strike didn't kill the poplar, but about half the tree was just gone, scattered all over the fields in big, long strips.

My 4'11" sister Jean and me at the horse trough.

The Time I Sang to the Calves

*T*he radio played a major role in my childhood. Most evenings after supper, Mother and Dad would send me out with a bowl to get apples from the cellar, which kept them crisp and cool, and we would eat the apples as we listened to the programs together. I remember listening to George Burns and Gracie Allen, *Fibber McGee and Molly*, and so many others. Another program I remember was an ongoing story about the Aldrich Family. It would usually start out with the mother going to the door and calling to her son: "Henrryyy! Henry Aldrich!" It was a funny program. Most of the radio programs were a half-hour long.

After school, I'd hurry to get my chores done so I could listen to kids' programs like *The Lone Ranger*. The announcer would say in his very dignified voice, "With pounding hoofs and a loud shout from the Lone Ranger, 'Hi ho, Silver, away'!"

Sitting by the radio, I was amazed by the sound effects. They were so real! I felt I was right there, and I could hardly wait for the next day to hear what was happening with the Lone Ranger and his Indian companion, Tonto. Each particular "episode" would last for a week. The announcer would say, "The Lone Ranger, champion of justice," and he would complete the program for that day with, "Goodbye until the next time." I used to take my horse out to the field and ride, playing at being the Lone Ranger or Tonto.

Another radio program was called *Major Bowes' Amateur Hour.* It would come on once a week and consisted of different people singing or playing musical instruments. It was kind of like the program we have now on the television, *America's Got Talent.*

Our calves had a shed to use for shelter when the weather was bad in winter, but in the middle of summer, the shed was usually empty. One night, I herded the calves into the shed and began my own personal musical performance for them. I knew a lot of songs because my sister, Jean, played the piano. She would get the sheet music for songs from different movies, and I would learn all the lyrics and sing as she was playing.

The moon was full that night. It was so bright that it was almost like daylight. The calves watched me as I sang to them, the moonlight glowing behind me. I saw my shadow as I stood at the open end of the shed and went from one song and dance to another. As the evening grew late, my mother came looking for me. I am sure that even from a distance, she could hear me belting out songs.

"What are you doing?" she asked, trying to keep a straight face.

"I'm playing *Major Bowes' Amateur Hour,*" I replied.

She laughed and laughed, and eventually, she told me it was late, and I needed to get back to the house. So I did.

The Chicken Whisperer

*O*ur garage was built into the side of a hill about twenty feet away from the chicken pen. The back of the garage was buried three or four feet into the hill. As I grew older, I got big enough to take hold of the side of the tin roof and climb to the top of the garage. I would then use the roof as a slide.

Our rooster hated me with a fiery passion. When he started to crow, I would try to mimic him. I had no idea what I was saying to him in "chicken language," but it was definitely mockery. He had it in for me. When I crowed at him, he would chase me, and I'd run for the garage roof to get away from him.

One time as this was going on, I was standing between the chicken pen and the garage and hadn't calculated my running area. I couldn't get the gate to the chicken pen open in time, and the rooster caught me. He hit me with enough force to knock me down and then went wild. He was *mad*. He scratched me with both feet, flogged me with his wings, and pecked at me.

My mother happened to be nearby. When I started screaming, she ran over and pulled the rooster off me. I was bleeding in several places. I had learned my lesson—it is not good to mock roosters. I don't remember crowing at him again.

However, I never lost my touch. To this day, I speak chicken very well. I can cackle and cluck with the best of them.

Several years later, after my husband and I were married, we supplemented our income by buying burlap gunnysacks and old car batteries to resell. At one ranch we visited, there were a bunch of chickens running loose in the barnyard. I started cackling at them like a hen: "Bock, bock, bawwwwwk," and they went wild. I don't know what I was saying, but they sure were excited about it!

Patsy on the back of the contented cow, Spot. In the background on the right is the garage in the side hill. There the rooster would chase me as I crowed at him. I would run and climb up on the back of the roof to try and get away from him.

The Night I Styled My Father

One evening, I asked my dad if I could comb his hair. I must have been six or seven at the time—old enough to reach his head while he was sitting in his favorite chair in the living room.

He was reading the newspaper. He distractedly replied, "Oh, I guess so." He didn't have a lot of hair on the top of his head, but there was enough for me to be inspired. I knew what I was going to do.

I went into the bathroom and got my mother's box where she kept all her hair things. With the help of some gel, I wrapped up Dad's hair in small metal rollers and clamped them in place. Some of the pieces were too short to roll properly, so I put them up in pin curls. Then I sat back to let it dry. Dad was absorbed in his newspaper and didn't realize what I had done to him.

About an hour later, there was a knock on our front door. Dad got up to see who it was. A neighbor had some questions for him, and they talked for several minutes at the door.

As Dad returned to his chair, I exclaimed, "Uh-oh! One of the rollers is falling out of your hair!"

Dad's hand jerked up. He felt the top of his head and groaned. "No wonder Harvey Chase kept staring at my head!"

Mother giggled. "He was probably looking at those rollers and pin curls!"

That was the last time Dad ever let me put rollers in his hair. I've always wondered what Harvey said to his wife when he got home.

The First Time I Felt God's Call

*R*anch work lasts seven days a week. My parents went to church only on Easter and Christmas, but when I was very young, Mother would sometimes take my sister and me to church and drop us off. She'd go home to make lunch for the hired hands and the rest of the family, and then she would come back and pick us up.

The church was near the Cedarville park. It was one of the original buildings in the town and looked like the church in *Little House on the Prairie*. Near the front of the room stood an old pump organ my sister would sometimes play while we waited for our mother. Jean was very good at playing the keyboard. I have fond memories of that church.

For instance, one Sunday when I was about five years old, I was standing next to my sister at the end of the meeting, and she started to cry. I started to cry, too, but I didn't know what was happening. I thought I was crying because she was crying—I didn't understand that it was the Holy Spirit touching me. Looking back, I recognize that I was feeling the presence of the Lord. My sister was a small person. She was only four feet eleven when she was fully grown. That day at church, I was small enough to look up at her and wonder what was going on with her.

The pastor asked people to come up to the front of the room if they wanted to give their hearts to Jesus. There was a padded

20

prayer bench where people could kneel and a railing that I gripped with both hands as I prayed the sinner's prayer and gave my heart to Jesus, but I didn't really know what I was doing. (It wasn't until my husband and I were dating that he took me to church and asked me what I didn't understand. I was in high school at that time, and God had His hand on me.)

On another Sunday morning, as my sister and I were walking into the church, we passed the bell rope, and I stopped the man who was about to pull it.

"Can I ring the bell?" I asked eagerly.

"All right," he replied, and lifted me up so I could reach the rope. It was such a thrill to ring the church bell and alert people all over the area that Sunday school was about to start. You could hear that bell all the way to our ranch two miles away.

The Time I Bit the Horse

*E*very summer, we used teams of draft horses to put up our hay for the winter. When I was five or six years old, my job was very important: Every day at noon while the men had lunch, I would water the horses one at a time at the horse trough.

One particular day, I was watering this draft horse named Ol' Pete. He was huge—I barely came up to his shoulder. I brought him to the trough, and he shifted his weight and set his hoof right on my bare foot. The area around the trough was muddy, so my foot sank instead of breaking beneath his weight. He had huge hooves, and I couldn't get him off me. I pushed him and screamed and cried. It hurt horribly, but no matter what I did, I couldn't get him to move. Draft horses weigh about a ton. They're big.

Finally, there was only one thing left to do. I had to bite him. I clamped my teeth down on his shoulder just above his leg. And he moved!

When I had finished watering all the horses, I stumbled back to the house with dirt, tears, and horsehair all over my face.

"What in the world happened to you?" my mother asked.

"Ol' Pete stepped on my foot," I said, "and the only thing I could think to do was bite him."

She looked at me in surprise. "Why did you bite him?"

"I pushed him, and he just leaned on me. I was stuck beneath his big old hoof!"

Mother checked my foot and washed my face. The horse never stepped on me again—I was much more careful. And, thankfully, I've never had the occasion to bite another horse.

Pasty atop the workhorse, Pete.

The Pesky Dam Builders. And the Scary Eagle

*Y*ou never know what sort of wildlife you'll come across on a ranch, so you have to be prepared. We experienced some odd things on our ranch in Cedarville.

One time during the summer, I was driving six or eight head of horses by myself from our home ranch to one my dad leased out of Eagleville. Our home ranch was about forty or fifty acres and it wasn't large enough to handle our growing herd of cattle. The ranch in Eagleville was larger and the cattle had to be down at that end of the valley anyway so that in the spring, they could be turned out onto the open range in Nevada. I would gallop the horses for a while, let them rest and walk or trot, and then gallop them again.

I was riding along the Warner mountain range when suddenly, a loud screech came out of the mountains. I stopped my horse under a cliff that loomed over my left side and listened, trying to locate what was making that sound.

I finally saw the noisemaker—it was an eagle trying to kill a mule-tailed deer fawn. The large bird would swoop down, pick it up in his talons, carry the fawn high into the air, and then drop it.

Disturbed, I hollered and tried to distract him, but it didn't work. The eagle did this about half a dozen times until the fawn was dead. Then he picked up the body and took it back to his nest. The stuff of nightmares, let me tell you, but that is how nature survives.

The Warner mountain range is filled with canyons and streams of water from the snow melting in the higher elevations. A creek flowed down from one of those canyons through our ranch, and we used the water to irrigate the alfalfa fields and a large garden out beyond the corral in front of the house. We had to have that water, but sometimes it would quit flowing.

Whenever that happened, my dad would say, "Oh, no. I'll have to go up in the canyon and break up a beaver dam."

There were years when he had to go break up the dams several times in a single summer because the beavers would rebuild them for raising their young. Dad was always in a hurry to get it done, and the dam was a good distance away. Pesky beavers. All's a fight between humans and the wild animals but, of course, animals were here first.

The Darn Sneaky Sheep

On the ranch we had horses, cattle, and a small herd of sheep, which my dad often assigned to my care. I had the job of moving them from one pasture to another. At seven years of age, I would go out on horseback and round up the sheep. I would start them up the lane and get them on the main road headed south toward Eagleville and a pasture my dad had rented.

But sheep are also easily frightened. Often as I was driving them into the next pasture, they would find a hole in the bordering fence only large enough for one sheep and sneak through it, contrary to where I wanted them to go. Predictably, if one sheep went, they all followed. Herding the sheep sometimes took me half a day or longer.

Dad would come along in his pickup, and I'd tell him, "The stupid sheep went through a hole in the fence."

I would ride my horse up the field and to herd them back out onto the road. By that time, they would have scattered in all directions, grazing on newfound brush and grass. We didn't have a sheepdog, but we sure could have used one.

Each evening, Dad had to go out and check on the sheep because sheep are pretty defenseless. If a sheep falls into a ditch, or even just lays down in one, you have to help it get up. If they get stuck on their backs, they just give up. Their organs don't work properly when they're upside down; it's difficult for them to breathe.

They're constantly in danger of being killed by coyotes. So Dad would always check on them for their own safety.

We had a good-sized ewe that bore twins every year, and several times, she even had triplets, which is pretty rare. Every year we had at least three or four bummer lambs. We called them that because they had to "bum" for milk as their mothers only had two nipples. Some first-time-mother ewes wouldn't accept their lambs and would even butt them when they would try to nurse. So we'd feed them cow's milk from an old ketchup or coke bottle strapped with a rubber nipple. I used to keep the bummer lambs for 4-H projects. I had a calf one time, too, but I didn't stay in 4-H very long because there was so much other ranch work to do.

God said it pretty well in the Bible! We are His sheep. The Bible is full of shepherds who had firsthand experience with sheep and their silly ways, and they understood what He was talking about. It's not very complimentary, but He loves us anyway.

Patsy with one of her "bummer" lambs. In the background is the tree that was struck by lightning.

The Thing I Will Never Do Again

One winter's day, my dad got a call from a neighbor who lived near us, up toward Lake City north of Cedarville. He had discovered two of our cows in with his cattle. This happens every so often when you keep your cattle out on an open range: Your livestock will get mixed up with somebody else's, and ranchers will give you call when they start separating out their herds. We had to call the neighbors once in a while, too, when we found some of their stray cows with ours. That is one reason ranchers brand or earmark their cattle—to be able identify them later out on open ranges.

My brother Earl and I took off to get the cattle. That particular day, the temperature was below zero, and with the added wind chill, it felt like it was twenty below. It was a clear day, but we were headed due north, and that north wind blowing made it miserable. It chilled you clear through. Even the horses didn't like to face into it.

The two feet of snow on the ground was capped with a two-inch hard layer of frozen snow that the horses' hooves would break through, and the jagged edges would sometimes skin them enough to draw blood. It was so cold that frost clung to our eyebrows, eyelashes, and the hair around the horses' mouths and nostrils.

I was wearing layers: long underwear, jeans, and chaps—we wore chaps a lot in the winter to help keep warm. I had a scarf, multiple sweaters, jackets, and gloves. I was so bundled up I couldn't bend my legs and had to get help mounting my horse.

The neighbor's range was about ten miles to the north. Earl and I didn't talk much, other than to say, "Hurry." Because we couldn't. We kept our bandanas pulled up around our faces like outlaws, trying to block that horrible north wind. I vaguely remember picking up the cattle—but mostly, I just remember the cold. The way back wasn't quite as bad because we weren't going into the wind anymore, as it was to our backs this time.

I made a mental note never to do that again.

Another time, two of our cows and a bull got mixed up with another rancher's herd at the other end of the valley near Eagleville, and Dad and I had to go get them. We did our buckerooing on the weekend when I wasn't in school so I could help him. ("Buckerooing" means moving cattle or horses—it's a general term for any work involving ranch animals.)

The day was cloudy. We had to ride down past our fence line near one of the alkali lakes to get out onto the open range. After we had retrieved the cattle, the bull took off by himself, and my dad went after him, leaving me with the two cows.

I got the cows turned around and headed home. But by that time, the fog had closed in, and we were facing into heavy rain and sleet. Eventually, I couldn't tell where we were. I knew I was going south, the direction of our ranch, because I was facing into the wind and the storm, which neither the animals nor I appreciated. The cows gave me a hard time.

In the rain, sleet, and fog, I could barely see the cows. I hollered for my dad, but he didn't holler back. Finally, when we got to the road and the fence, I knew we were on the right trail back home. Dad arrived with the bull about the same time I did and we headed for the safety of the ranch house.

The Parade with All the Blood

*M*y family raised a few horses. We were cattle people, but like every little cowgirl, I adored horses. Once, with my horse Pepper, I entered the Western Trail class at school, which was always important to me.

It was a horse show. First, you rode your animal around in a circle, and then you would get off your horse, lay the reins on the ground, and walk away. If your horse didn't follow you, it meant he was "ground tied," and that was good. The horse wouldn't move until you went back and took the reins.

My problem was getting back in the saddle. I wasn't tall enough to put my foot in the stirrup, so my dad taught me a way to get back up on my horse all by myself: At the end of the reins is a romal, which is a Spanish word for "whip." "Throw the romal up over your saddle horn," he said, "and then you can pull your body up to get your foot into the stirrup."

At the next show, the announcer said, "Let's watch this little girl. How is she going to get up on that tall horse?"

I threw the romal over the saddle horn and pulled myself up to where my foot could reach the stirrup. Everybody started cheering. "She made it!" It was one of my prouder moments.

Most of the horses in Surprise Valley were mustangs—wild horses pulled off the range and bred with draft horses, which made a pretty poor combination for working with cattle. So one year, my dad purchased a palomino stallion from his friend in San Jose to improve the quality of the valley horses. The stallion was part Arabian and part Morgan, and we named him Modoc after our county.

On July 4, 1940, my dad was asked to take our stallion over to an annual Fourth of July parade in Alturas. In those days, no one had horse trailers to transport their animals. Most ranchers could barely afford a pickup or an old car; the Great Depression had left people in a pretty bad way.

As it turned out, another rancher was in the process of building a horse trailer. He wasn't quite through with it yet, but my dad was able to borrow it so we could get Modoc to the parade. The trailer looked a little like a wagon because it didn't have a top; it was completely open, and the rancher had left very sharp, unfinished metal strips along the top edges. In the front of the trailer, there was a manger with a metal pipe where you could tie up the halter rope.

We arrived in Alturas early to get ready for the parade. Modoc had been well groomed before we left our ranch, but it was a twenty-five mile trip from Cedarville, so, of course, he was not well groomed when we arrived. He had green manure all over his tail and legs, and I had to get him all washed up and clean for the parade.

I hadn't been told anything about the parade except that I was riding in it. After I had cleaned up the horse, a man came by in his pickup and my dad told me to get in. The man was the parade coordinator.

When we got to a certain street, he started giving me instructions. "When you get to this corner, turn here."

I was listening, but I wasn't sure why he was telling me all of this. I finally asked, and he replied, "You are going to be leading the parade!"

I thought I could remember most of the turns, and if I missed some, I figured it really wouldn't matter much—what can you

31

expect from an eight-year-old girl who wasn't warned in advance? We returned to the horse and saddled up, and I positioned myself at the front of the parade.

The band started to play, and I nudged the horse forward up the street. People applauded. The announcer blared over the speaker, "Look at that beautiful horse and that little girl riding him!" I had a wonderful time.

In the afternoon when the rodeo was over, we loaded Modoc in the trailer. He was a little anxious to get home—he'd had a busy day. Around five o'clock, as we were going up the winding road that leads to Cedar Pass, Modoc decided he'd had enough and tried to jump out of the trailer. His head was tied to the metal pipe, but there was some slack in the rope, and he managed to get a leg over the side of the trailer.

Dad stopped the truck, and we both jumped out. The horse thrashed about and struggled in a complete panic. There was blood everywhere because Modoc had cut himself on the unfinished metal strips running along the trailer. They were as sharp as knives.

My dad grabbed his pocketknife and cut the lead rope off the trailer while dodging horse hooves. It took only a few minutes, but it seemed like forever. We managed to get the horse out of the trailer

Patsy on Modoc, Fourth of July Parade in Alturas County, 1940.

and calm him down. He had barely missed cutting a large artery under his belly.

Modoc was so spooked over the ordeal that we couldn't put him back in the trailer, and there was no way of getting him home other than to ride him. After we got most of the bleeding to stop, I told Dad, "I'll ride him."

"You sure?" he said.

"I'll be all right," I replied.

So we saddled him up, and Dad followed along behind me with the pickup and trailer. It was a little more than fifteen miles, and after a while, Dad went on ahead to drop off the trailer, but he came back to see how we were doing. When I told him we were fine, he went home.

Periodically, I stopped to make sure the bleeding hadn't started again. Whenever a car or truck passed us, the drivers would stop in a flurry of concern.

"Are you all right? What happened?" were the most frequently asked questions.

I suppose it was pretty odd to see a young child spattered with blood, riding a bloody horse down the side of the road. I was leading my second parade of the day! People kept stopping and staring, and they wouldn't let me leave. It was getting late, and I needed to get home. Everyone wanted to know what had happened, and finally, I almost had to be rude. "I have to get home! It's getting dark!" I finally exclaimed.

As the sun set in the west, I urged Modoc into a trot because I didn't want to ride along the road in the dark. Close to the house, I pushed him into a gallop, and we finally arrived safe at home.

Horse Roundup at
Its Finest

*N*owadays, some people have problems with deer that eat their gardens, or coyotes that kill their chickens, or maybe a wild dog or two. In the 1940s, ranchers in northern California had all these problems plus one that might take you by surprise— wild horses. They would eat the grass on the cattle ranges, which I suppose they still do.

I'm not sure how the wild horses got to Surprise Valley. I think when the early settlers came, they probably turned their horses out on the range, and some of them were never gathered back up. To this day, there are still wild horses out in the desert. They round them up in Nevada and sell them in auction in Red Bluff.

When I was about seven years old, Lois Miller was a good friend of mine. We were classmates. Her family lived in Nevada, but they also had a house in town, where Lois and her mom stayed during the week so Lois could go to school. Then in the summer, they would go back to their ranch in Nevada.

One summer, I spent a week with Lois on her parents' ranch. The mares had foals that spring, and Lois told me that her dad, Buzz, wanted to capture the wild stallion that had joined up with the broodmares. There were also some stray mares in this group that her dad wanted to corral, either to sell them or to increase his herd of broodmares.

Since it was late summer, it was time to bring the mares and foals off the range in preparation for winter. Buzz had been out on the range the week before and knew the general area where they were, which was important because you don't want to waste your time or your horse's energy.

Early in the morning, the three of us went out to hunt them down. We were still several miles away when the stallion saw us coming. The land was all open cattle range, full of sagebrush, and the stallion shot off in a wild run.

Buzz raced after him and a couple of the mares. My dad had taught me years before not to gallop my horse through rocky terrain because the horse could stumble and fall, potentially rolling on top of me. But the horses we were riding had been raised in this area. They knew how to navigate the rocky land.

Buzz gained ground and separated from us to follow the stallion and the two mares he had taken with him. Lois and I took after the other mares and foals. We had to run quite a distance to get around them and head them off. But as the foals began to tire, they started to slow, and the rest of the herd began to quiet down. We eventually got around them and herded them back to the ranch. We were young kids, but you learn to do this type of work when you're growing up on a ranch. You just see other people doing it, and you learn. A seven- or eight-year-old can be very helpful in that way.

I think more than half of the horses were Buzz's, and the rest were wild. We had run for almost ten miles to capture them. Lois and I followed the setting sun west.

Buzz finally had to let the stallion and a handful of mares go because they got way ahead of him, and his horse was getting tired. We were a long ways from the ranch, and we had to get the other mares and foals back.

When we reached the ranch, the mares and foals were put in a field where they could water and graze. There were quite a few of them. Each mare had a foal. We unsaddled our horses, turned them loose in the corral, and threw some hay out for them.

Lois's mom had fixed us a great big dinner of steak and potatoes with lots of vegetables. All that good food for our long day's work.

L to R: Patsy, Brothers Bud and Earl, and Dad getting ready for a round up.

The Unconscious Calf

One night, my brother Bud came in late after herding cattle or doing some other ranch activity. Mother had dinner waiting for him.

Both my brothers often called me "Sam" because I felt sorry for a rodeo bronc rider named Sam Asher. The man was always getting thrown off his horse in the rodeos.

"Sam," Bud said, "when I get through eating, I got something down in the barn for you."

"What is it, Bud? What is it?"

"Well, wait," he replied. "Let me eat."

When he was finished eating, he took a flashlight down to the side of the barn where we kept the horses, and standing there blinking at us was a type of foal we called a leppy. Evidently, he hadn't had enough milk to drink during his growth time because he was stunted, like the runt of a litter, about the size of a pony.

"Oh! Is he mine?" I asked.

"Yeah," Bud replied. "I'll let you have him."

I called the foal Brown Jug, and I helped raise and halter break him.

Bud had brought the motherless foal home from the range because there was no brand on him. We had no way of knowing which ranch the foal was from, so he couldn't be returned.

That's why you brand—so you can identify your livestock. People have tried to mark cattle and horses in ways that don't involve heating up the branding iron, but it takes too much time. If you have a hundred or more head of calves to brand, you can't be fooling around doing little things. When city people hear about branding, they rise up and cry, "You're hurting them! Abusing the cattle!" Well, city folk just don't know how easy it is to lose your livelihood on the open range. The livestock are what you live and work for. It's not cruel, it is common sense.

One year, we were down at the Papst Ranch (the one my father had rented in Eagleville), and it was time to brand our spring calves. Granddad Grove (my mother's dad) was doing the roping from his horse, and my dad and brother would take each calf, put it on the ground, and brand it. The brand doesn't always go on the back hip, like you see in the movies. The placement of the brand depends on the state you live in and whatever permissions it gives. We usually branded calves along the ribs on the right side.

In the cowboy movies, you'll see your "traditional" brands, like the Rocking R and things like that. For some reason, my dad marked his cattle with his initials. He could have used the initials of his first and middle names—*Burt Harrison*—but no, he apparently had to have *Burt Simpson*, so all our cattle and horses were branded with a very noticeable "BS."

That particular year, we had a calf that was a little bit larger than some of the others. My dad and brother got through ear-marking and branding him and turned him loose, as they had the rest of the calves. Nobody was paying attention to this calf, who was so angry at what had happened to him that he ran into back end of my granddad's horse. The horse threw off my granddad and kicked the calf in the skull hard enough to knock it out.

My dad and brother thought the horse had killed the calf, but it was only unconscious. But my granddad was furious. Getting thrown had startled him. He got down beside the unconscious calf and rubbed manure in its face, and then they dragged it out of the corral.

My sister-in-law happened to be sitting on the top fence rail with a camera while all this was going on, and that's how we ended up with the picture we took of the hard-headed calf.

The unconscious calf & branding cattle.

The Eight-Year-Old Pickup Driver

I learned to drive a pickup when I was just a kid. We lived in a remote area where there was hardly any traffic. I sat in my dad's lap as he taught me how to steer, and he would push the clutch in and show me how to shift the gears. I was so small that I could see out the windshield only by peeking through the slats of the steering wheel.

One day, Granddad Grove and I were going down to Papst Ranch. I got into the driver's seat, and Granddad asked me, "Don't you want me to drive?"

I was only eight years old at the time. "Oh, no," I replied lightly. "Dad lets me drive all the time."

Granddad was pretty apprehensive as we started the seventeen-mile trip to Eagleville, and his concern only got worse. We came to a slight turn in the road, and I hit it too fast. The pickup went into a sideways skid in the gravel. This was before seatbelts; I hung on to the steering wheel, but my granddad ricocheted around the truck cab!

With an expression of sheer terror, his eyes popping out of his head, he asked me again, "Don't you want me to drive?!"

"No, I'm fine," I replied.

I was determined to stay behind the wheel, but I heartily failed to impress my granddad with my skills.

The Egg Thieves

*M*y mother raised chickens for food and to trade the eggs for groceries at the store. Once or twice a year, she would order the chicks from a hatchery down in the Sacramento Valley, and they would be delivered by mail. The post office would call our old crank phone to tell us the chickens had arrived, and we had to come pick them up because their chirping was driving everyone crazy.

Dad had built Mother a nice chicken house that could hold about fifty baby chicks. On one side was a 2x4 roost with a little ladder that the chicks could use as they got older. It wasn't a chicken *coop*, which is a small shelter, but an actual chicken *house*. It was completely covered, the way a house would be.

Each spring, Mother would muck out the old manure from the year before and scrub down the inside of the building. I remember her mixing up water and a white, chalky powder that turned into something she called whitewash, but it wasn't paint. She'd put it in a spray can and spray down the interior of the henhouse, so it would be nice and clean for the new chicks. It even smelled clean after she got done with it. The whitewash didn't really sterilize anything, but it covered up what had been there before.

Mother ordered fifty chicks at a time, and they came in two boxes, each about two feet long by two feet wide, that had little dividing walls inside so it was harder for the chicks to get mashed.

Baby chicks are pretty frail, but there wasn't too much danger as they traveled from the hatchery to the post office.

We would take the fluffy yellow chicks out of the box one by one. The first step was getting them hydrated, but it was a bit tricky because they were so little that they hadn't learned how to drink yet. You'd hold onto their wings and feet, take their head, dip their beak into a dish of water, and sort of scoop water into their mouth. Then you'd tilt the chick back a little bit in your hand so the water would go down their throat, and they'd learn how to swallow. We did this with all fifty chicks. Some would catch on pretty quickly and would go back for more water on their own. Others we had to help a second time.

Even in the spring, when the chicks arrived, it would still get plenty cold in Surprise Valley. So after watering the chicks, we would place them under the flap of the brooder to keep them warm. A brooder was a round contraption heated by a kerosene burner in the center of the top. The walls were canvas curtain, like a circus tent, and the chicks were able to go in and out. They didn't have to stay in there all the time, but we wouldn't let them out of the chicken house until they were a little bigger. They were always really small when they first arrived, and we would have to take good care of them.

Usually, the baby chicks recovered from their mail trip overnight, and the next morning, we'd introduce them to chicken mash, a powdered grain that my mother would mix with a little water so the chicks could eat it better. As they grew, they would learn to eat it dry.

We'd have to keep an eye on them because the mean ones—the little juvenile delinquent chicks—would start pecking the others, and they could kill them. This went on even as they got older. They could pluck all the feathers off one their clan mates and start chasing it around. We'd have to separate them sometimes and put them in different pens.

We had two chicken houses, one for the new chicks and one for our older residents (the laying hens). Dad built nests for the hens, and we lined the nests with straw so they had a nice place to lay their eggs. The houses had doors on either end with little ramps leading out into the separate pens so the chickens could go in and out and run around. At night, all Mother had to do was close the little doors, and we wouldn't have any problems with animals getting in and killing the chickens.

The main things we had to watch for were crows and magpies. During the day, when the little doors were open, the magpies could fly into the pen, march up the little ramp, and steal the eggs. They were pretty crafty. We would often see magpies walking down the ramp with eggs in their beaks. My dad kept a .410-gauge shotgun by our front door near the coatrack to help control the egg thieves.

The first time my mother heard the magpies screeching, she ran to save her eggs. She loaded the shotgun but didn't check to see if the safety was on first. The gun went off in the house and blew a hole in the kitchen roof. So the next time she went after the egg thieves, she went outside before loading the gun.

She shot one of the magpies, took the body, and hung it by baling wire in the apricot tree that stood in the corner of the pen. We'd been having quite a problem with the magpies—until Mother hung that dead bird in the tree. The magpies gathered around their fallen comrade and squawked their mourning.

The egg-thieving slowly diminished after that. Mother left the dead bird in the tree, and it worked for a long time.

The moral of the story is: There are few things in ranch life you can't solve with a .410 shotgun and a little bit of bailing wire.

The Barn Tragedy

When alfalfa gets a bloom on it, it's ready to be cut for hay. When I was still pretty little, nobody had tractors. Instead, we used teams of horses to help with the haying. You'd hitch the team to a mowing machine that had a long sickle on it. The machine's gears would swing the sickle back and forth as the wheels turned, and the cut hay would fall in straight swaths.

The first cut made a path for you to follow as you went around the field. Sometimes, you'd have to back up the horses and the mowing machine to unclog it because the hay got tangled up in the sickle bar. Clover is an especially mean old plant. Clover seeds ball up and make huge clumps of grass around the sickle bar. In my childhood, I spent a lot of time backing up horses to unclog the sickle bar.

On a ranch, you learn pretty quick what you should and shouldn't do, and here's the thing about hay—it's fickle. You have to let it dry completely before you do anything with it, even just stack it. If you put it up before it's dry, it likes to catch on fire.

Neighbors helped neighbors when they had a need, and putting up the first crop was a big one. One day when I was about seven or eight, we were helping a neighbor, Mr. Steiner, put up his alfalfa. He thought his hay was ready to be put into the barn, where he stored it to feed his dairy cows and horses.

It had been in the barn for about a week when, in the middle of the night, a fire siren went off in town, waking all of us up. When we arrived at Mr. Steiner's place, his barn was completely consumed in flames. Animals were shrieking inside, and thick smoke was pouring from the roof.

We tried to get the livestock out of the barn, but the horses were spooked and confused. As soon as we released them, they bolted back into the burning barn. Horses get spooked in fires. The barn is their home, and they think they will be safe there.

More neighbors came to help put out the fire, and the fire truck arrived, but there wasn't anything we could do. Mr. Steiner lost not only his barn but also some pigs and other animals. I don't think he lost everything—I was too young to remember—but he lost a lot.

"The hay we put in the barn wasn't completely dry," my dad told me later. It had formed a combustible gas and flared up, taking the barn and animals with it.

Fire was just one of the dangers ranchers needed to accept and endure, part and parcel of the lifestyle. So Mr. Steiner didn't give up. He just kept on ranching. He'd lost his hay for the animals, but I believe some neighbors helped rebuild his barn and replenish his hay supply. That was what neighbors did to help one another. Of course that type of help goes on today when a tragedy happens; hurricanes, earthquakes and other natural disasters bring out the compassion God has placed in our hearts for our fellow human beings.

Stacking hay using nets, cables and pulleys.

Our Pet Canada Geese

One day as Dad was walking through one of our meadows, he happened to see a nest of Canada geese. The chicks were very small, and he decided to bring two of them home.

Mother took a pan of chicken mash and added some water to see if she could get the goslings to eat. She treated them as she would baby chicks. Taking hold of their little legs and bodies, she scooped the wet mash into their mouths, and they took to eating it very quickly. After the first taste, they were on their own.

We kept them in the chicken house when they were small, but as they grew, they were allowed to wander the yard. They loved us and would follow us, like dogs would. At night, they crawled under Dad's pickup for shelter. They bonded with that pickup and would follow it into town, flying beside the window. It got to where, after they were older, they would fly beside us into Cedarville when we went to the post office and land in the street. As we left town, they would *honk, honk, honk* around the truck and return to the ranch with us. At that point, we had to clip their wings to keep them from getting hit by a car. Feathers grow the way hair does; when clipped, they eventually grow back.

After a few years, our geese disappeared as the wild geese migrated through our area. We guessed that they joined up with them to live on their own and do what geese do. But it was a fun experience to have them living on the ranch with us.

The Way God Preserved Our Finances

When I was a child, hardly anyone talked to their children about finances. It was only a few years after the stock market crash of 1929. One day at school, my classmate, Pauline, whose parents owned the lumberyard, came up to me and said, "My parents say your parents are rich."

I didn't know anything about that. My parents never spoke about it. I knew they bought a new car or a pickup every year, or every other year, but that was the extent of my understanding of money.

So I asked my mother about it. "Pauline says we're rich."

My mother got mad. "We're *not* rich, and don't you ever say that again!" she replied. She and Dad didn't like people knowing about their finances, even though it was very evident that we did have money. Nobody else we knew could buy a new car every year.

My parents bought the first automatic washing machine, a Bendex, in Surprise Valley. Women from town would come down to see how this new machine worked. It was a front loader with a window so you could see the clothes tumbling over and over in the sudsy water. I remember one of the women asking my mother, "What do you do when the clothes are washing?"

"Well, I just go on with the rest of my housework," my sensible mother politely replied.

I still think that was a strange question. I guess the lady thought my mother sat down and watched the clothes being washed!

Dad also bought my mother an ironing machine, which she could set down and iron all the men's shirts on. She got very expert at doing this. She also ironed sheets, pillowcases, etc. She would let me iron Dad's handkerchiefs; there was a lever that she would push with her knee, which raised the hot surface and pressed the material flat.

My parents were very progressive for the era they lived in. Often they would deviate from the current trends, improving our lives in many ways.

As I told you, my dad bought Modoc, the palomino stallion, so he could improve the quality of the mustang horses. He and my mother also did a lot of different things to the house. They put a yard in and surrounded it with an ornate wire fence. Mother loved to plant shrubs and flowers and other things, so the yard was all fixed up with a rock garden—common today, but not so common for the times they lived in.

My family was able to purchase items even during hard times because my dad had gotten his money out of the bank before the stock market crash. He had what my mother called a "premonition" and removed his savings because of it. Later, the bank run started, and you couldn't get anything out.

That is how God protected our finances. Even though my father wasn't a Christian at the time, God still moved in his heart to keep our family going during the Great Depression.

The Attack on Pearl Harbor

*T*he day the Japanese bombed Pearl Harbor, my family was sitting at the kitchen table eating breakfast. We were listening to the Sunday morning news on the radio when the broadcast was interrupted.

"Pearl Harbor has been attacked," the announcer said. "The Japanese bombed the harbor and continued the shooting in the hills above Pearl City." The announcer said Wheeler Airfield in Honolulu had been attacked as well.

I was nine years old at the time, and I still remember the fright and shock everyone around the breakfast table felt. I asked, "Are they coming here to bomb us?"

"No," my parents answered, but everyone was apprehensive at the news.

World War II changed a lot of things for us. Along with the war came rationing on items like shoes (the leather had to be saved for the war effort—for shoes for the soldiers), silk stockings, gas, sugar, butter, and many other things as well. The government sent out ration books that contained a certain number of ration stamps, which allowed you to get what you needed but no more. Gas and tires were rationed, too, but because we lived on a ranch and were raising food, we were allowed extra gas coupons and extra tires.

For the most part, the war didn't keep us from doing normal, everyday things, and one day, we went down to my great-aunt

Lilly's house in San Francisco. She was a loud, flamboyant lady and a wonderful great-aunt to me. Whenever we went to visit her, we'd always go out to see a Broadway show and have dinner at a nice restaurant. The government was rationing sugar, but that didn't stop Aunt Lilly from getting as much as she wanted—she had a big purse. At the restaurant, she stealthily dumped the sugar cubes off the table into her purse and sneaked them home with her! It was very funny, and I am still laughing about it now.

At school, we could purchase war stamps. Each morning before class, right after we said the Pledge of Allegiance, Mrs. Hill and Mrs. Wiley would ask if anyone wanted to buy war stamps. When the books were full, the stamps could be turned into war bonds, which would gain interest during the war and could be cashed in later. After my husband and I were married, I cashed in my war bonds. The first amount was a $25.00 bond to help buy cows for our dairy.

My family didn't go without much during the war, but my folks did have to stop buying a new car every year.

The Time Earl
Nearly Killed Us

*M*y brother Earl was always fascinated with planes. He loved building model airplanes and had a bunch of different models that kept getting bigger and bigger. Eventually, he made a model airplane that was almost big enough for me to sit in, and I wanted to sit in it so bad! But he wouldn't let me.

"No," he said, "you'll break it."

The model was made of balsam wood—that really lightweight wood they still make models with—but it had a little gasoline engine that allowed it to fly. He would take the plane out to one of the alkali lakes near the ranch and fly it around. Model airplanes didn't have great controls the way they do now, but when it ran out of gas, it would catch the thermals and float down softly. When it eventually landed, it wouldn't suffer too much damage. It had about a six-foot wingspan. If there had just been a little more room in the cockpit, I could have climbed in! Earl still loves his planes.

After the Japanese attacked Pearl Harbor, Earl wanted to join the Air Force. He had already attended the aeronautical school in Santa Monica, so he had more experience than some. The closest Air Force recruiting station was in Klamath Falls, Oregon. When Earl decided to enlist, it was the middle of winter, and the roads were icy. On the way back from Klamath Falls, Earl was driving our new 1940 wine-colored Chevrolet sedan, the last new car we would have for a while because of the war. My dad was sitting beside Earl, and my mother and I were in the backseat.

We came over a rise, and Earl saw another car coming. We had plenty of room between us and the oncoming car, but for some reason, Earl put on the brakes, which is the *wrong* thing to do on black ice, and our car went into a violent skid that flipped us over. We slammed into the embankment on the right side of the road with enough momentum that the car flipped again and landed on its wheels.

In the wreck, Mother was thrown into left corner of the backseat, and I was thrown to the right. This was long before cars were required to have seat belts. As the car stopped moving, I looked over at her, and her big black felt hat, which she wore when she dressed up, had fallen down over her face. Everybody was disheveled.

My dad turned around and looked at us, making sure we were all right. Then he straightened his hat and glared at my brother. "Why did you put your foot on the brake!? You know better than to hit the brakes."

Earl sheepishly looked back at Mom and me tossed around in the backseat.

It turned out that the accident wasn't too bad, but the frame of the car was sprung and it made the tires go all caddiwhompas. We limped the car home slowly. I'm pretty sure my dad drove the rest of the way—he was really mad because he knew we wouldn't be able to get a new car. No one was selling them because everything was going toward the war effort. We had to use the car in that same condition until we moved from Cedarville to San Jose **in 1944,** where my dad purchased a fairly new Plymouth coupe.

The Jerky and the Shoe

*I*n the fall during deer season, my dad, brothers, and Dr. Pate—our family doctor—would go hunting in Nevada. The deer in that part of the country spend a lot of time foraging in the sagebrush, so venison gets a distinct sage flavor.

Jerky was our primary food whenever we were out working on horseback. Mother prepared jerky by cutting the venison into thin strips and laying them on a long platform covered by a sheet under the clothesline. Dad built the platform for her because she was short, and she needed help reaching the drying line. It was a circular clothesline dad made for hanging. It was fairly large, too, in order to hold all the clothes for seven people.

In order to preserve the meat in those years, jerky was heavily salted and peppered and covered with cheesecloth netting to keep the flies off. At the end of the day, the jerky and the net were rolled up together in a sheet and stored in the cellar. Each morning, the bundle was carried outside again and laid out on the platform so the jerky could continue to dry and cure—a process that took weeks. After it was cured, we stuffed it into containers we carried with us when we went out buckarooing.

When we drove the cattle, we would snack on this meat. Due to the high salt content, I would make my dad stop in order to drink the water I needed after eating on the trail. I remember on one of the drives, I rode all the way to the hot springs near Cedarville and I was so thirsty, I drank straight out of the springs, hot water and all!

I was too little to go hunting with my dad and brothers, but I would go fishing with them. One day, Dad, my Uncle Louis (he was my mother's brother) and I headed up to Oregon to a good trout stream above the valley. We had never fished together before. All of us picked different points on the stream. I'd fish in one hole; my dad would fish in another, and Uncle Louis would post himself further upstream.

As I was crossing the water, I stumbled upon a hole in the streambed. The rocks along the streambed were slimy with moss, and I lost my footing. The hole was almost deep enough for me to swim in, and when I picked myself up, I no longer had my fishing rod. I looked all around for it and couldn't find it. It had floated downstream somewhere.

Dripping wet, I walked back to where my dad was.

"I dropped the pole," I said. "I can't find it."

He scowled at me. "That pole belonged to your uncle."

And then he noticed the pole wasn't the only thing I'd lost. One of my shoes was missing, too. He was not pleased.

During World War II, shoes were rationed, and you had to have shoe stamps in order to purchase them. You could buy only so many pairs a year, and my parents had just bought that pair for me. To this day, I don't know how I lost it. It's possible I stripped them off to go barefoot across the stream and accidentally lost one of them after falling in the water.

The Year Everything Changed

When I was in the seventh grade **1944,** my dad had a heart attack. I don't know many of the details because my parents didn't tell me much about it. I was still a little kid, and they didn't want me to worry. The only thing I knew was that my dad could die unless he made drastic life changes.

"The best thing to do is get out of the high altitude and away from heavy work," the doctor said. Both Dr. Pate and Dr. Kennedy advised my dad to sell the ranch and get out of the high altitude so there wouldn't be as much strain on his heart.

The only medication they had for him at the time was nitroglycerin. Dad called them his "little dynamite pills," and he always carried them in his shirt pocket. We started the process of selling the ranch and the equipment, and I helped my mother pack things up in the house.

For my parents, selling the ranch was like saying goodbye to one of their children. My family had lived there since 1924. As we packed, Mother often broke down in tears because she and Dad had practically homesteaded the place. They were uprooting everything—their entire lives. The ranch in Cedarville was the only home I'd ever known.

My parents and I loaded up everything and went down to San Jose to stay for a while with my mother's brother Raymond and his family.

My brother Bud and his wife, Marge, lived on in Cedarville at the ranch until it sold. It was the end of an era.

Culture Shock

*M*y uncle in San Jose was named Raymond, but no one ever called him that. Everybody called him Buzz. "Why do they call him Buzz?" I asked my mother, figuring it had something to do with bees.

She replied, "In big families, the little children can't say *brother*. They end up saying *buzzer* instead." And that was where he got his name. I never called him anything but Uncle Buzz.

While we were staying with Uncle Buzz and Aunt Esther, my dad bought a Spanish-style house in San Jose. It was a really nice house, with hardwood floors instead of linoleum, but there were renters in it when we bought it, and during World War II, you couldn't evict people. You had to give them six months to get out, and it ended up that we never did move into that house. By the time the people renting it finally left, we had other plans. Mother cried when we walked through the San Jose house one last time. She would have loved to live in that house because it was such a nice place.

We spent several weeks in San Jose with my uncle's family. As it became apparent that the nice house my dad had purchased wasn't going to work out, our plans changed. Dad was a rancher at heart, and he was still looking for one that he could buy and work on. Aunt Esther suggested we move in with her mother, who lived in a large, three-story Victorian house in Los Gatos where she leased out her grape vineyard. The leaser, however, didn't use the large

58

winery next to the house, and for the six months we lived with her, the winery was an interesting playland for me. It housed wine vats that were about fourteen feet long and twelve feet high, with ladders attached to them. It was a wonderful place for a kid to explore when not in school.

At the time, Los Gatos was only grape vineyards and apricot orchards. It was quite an adjustment for me, because I was used to high desert country that supported cattle, horses, and sheep. Modoc, our palomino stallion, had been sold to a family friend who lived in San Jose, so I was able to visit him on the weekends and go riding. It wasn't the same as riding on the ranch back home, but it did help ease my culture shock. Los Gatos was nothing like Surprise Valley.

There were some unpleasant surprises in store for me personally. Besides missing my birthplace, attending school in San Jose was a nightmare. I was a ranch kid from a small town in Surprise Valley, and I was unprepared for the size of the Willow Glen Junior High School. I had started the seventh grade in Cedarville, a class made up of five girls and six boys. The school itself had only four classrooms. But after a month attending the school in Cedarville, I had to pick up and move to Willow Glen, which had a thousand students, and when the bell rang, you changed rooms! I had seen this only in the movies. It still makes me cringe when I think about attending junior high in San Jose. I was forever getting lost trying to find my classes and I felt so alone.

Before my parents arranged for me to take the bus, my dad would drive me back and forth to school. He'd park in front of the school while I sat in the car and cried.

"Get out of the car, Pat," my father would firmly state.

I would hang onto the door handle and whimper, "I don't want to." I would stubbornly sit on the seat, clinging tightly to the handle.

My dad would finally lose his patience. "Pat, get out of the car, or I'm going to push you out."

One day, a girl saw all of this happening, and after my dad had driven away, she came up to me and said. "I think you are in all of my classes. Just stay with me, and I'll help you."

I was so relieved. After days and days of getting lost and dreading school, the process finally became manageable for me because of this girl. I don't remember her name, but I will always remember her. You never know how one little act of kindness will help alleviate somebody's trauma. It's always encouraging when complete strangers show love and mercy, and God shows His love by those acts of kindness.

The Tiny Seed

"And another parable put he forth to them, saying 'The kingdom of heaven is like a grain of mustard seed, which a man took, and sowed in his field, which indeed, is the least of all seeds, but when it is grown it is the greatest among herbs, and becometh a tree, so that the birds of the air come and lodge in the branches of it.' "

—*Matthew 13:31-32*

*D*ad wanted to find a ranch where he could speculate in cattle: buy them, fatten them up, and sell them for a profit. But down in San Jose and Los Gatos, there was no such thing. It was all orchards and vineyards. There were no cattle ranches, and ranching was all my dad knew. He wasn't sure where we should move, but there was one thing he did know—there was no way he was moving to the Sacramento Valley because of the heat.

As we drove through it, he declared, "If there is one place we are not going to live, it is the Sacramento Valley!"

I remember his exact words. They still resonate in my mind all these years later. When we lived in Cedarville, we avoided the Sacramento Valley whenever we traveled down to see Uncle Buzz and Aunt Esther because it was so hot in the summer. Cars didn't have air conditioning back then, and some still had to be started with a hand crank—they only started if you had a good, strong right arm!

Surprise Valley had hot weather, too, but with an elevation of 4,500 feet, "hot" weather was about 90 degrees Fahrenheit. But hot weather in the Sacramento Valley was 100 or 115 degrees or more. Big difference!

Dad wasn't able to find a ranch close by, so he began to venture farther and farther north, fnally ending up twenty miles outside of a town called Willows. There, finally, he spotted cattle, horses, and other livestock out the car window, so he stopped, contacted a realtor, and bought a ranch near the Sacramento River in an area called Ord Bend. My mother and I teased him because the ranch was in the Sacramento Valley—the very place he said he never wanted to be.

The school in Ord Bend was the third one I attended that year. It was even smaller than the school in Cedarville, and it was a relief for me to be back out in the country again with a smaller, closer community. I was happy to be back in the ranching world, and I am pretty sure my father was relieved as well.

Our new ranch bordered an irrigation canal that flowed from the newly built Shasta Dam. Water for irrigation was no problem, but the large house on the property needed some restoration and updates. It didn't have electricity, as the power lines ended about three miles from the ranch. The walls were plastered, and like older houses of the time, all the wood trim was stained a dark brown, almost black. The high plaster ceilings were "decorated" (I use that word loosely) with large wooden frames, so there were big squares everywhere.

My mother came in, looked around, and made a list of all the work that had to be done—the painting, the redecorating, sanding and varnishing the floors, laying down new linoleum, and she would have to take care of me besides. The task seemed impossible.

As we worked on the big house, Dad rented a small house close by; a "country block" (half a mile) down the road. The rental was a terrible place. It didn't have electricity, either, and I had to do all my schoolwork by lantern light.

As my dad got acquainted with some of the local ranchers, he found out that the best crop to raise was ladino clover seed. World War II was still in progress, and the government encouraged ranchers to grow clover seed because it was used to polish bomber cylinders. Farmers who raised clover seed were paid a subsidy. In the midst of painting the house, taking care of the clover crops, and growing and watering a field of alfalfa for hay for the livestock, there was not a spare moment.

I was the one who cut the clover seed crop because I was the only one with the time. My brother Earl was in the Air Force until the war ended, but my brother Bud and his family moved to the ranch in Ord Bend after my parents' ranch in Cedarville sold. So we all worked the land together.

The night before I'd go out with the tractor, I would take a grease gun and grease up the mowing machine. Then I would get up the next morning at four o'clock, when the dew was still heavy so the delicate seed was moist and wouldn't fall out of the seed head, and head out with the tractor. Clover isn't the easiest plant to deal with. I constantly had to back the tractor up, hop off the seat, clear the sickle bar of giant balls of stems and seed pods, then start the process over again. The sickle bar had blades on it, and the seed with all the stems and leaves would get wound up on the sickle bar. I was backing up the tractor as much as I was rolling forward in the harvesting process.

All of this was done in the dark. When the sun came up, I was done with mowing the clover for the day because the dew would dry, and the clover seeds would become loose and fall out if handled. When the entire field was cut, the clover seed would be left to dry in the sun for a day or two. Then I'd go out at the same early morning hour and attach a side delivery rake to the tractor. Starting at one end of the field, I would make windrows (long lines) of the seed until the whole field was completed, and the harvester could come pick up the seed.

The harvester was sort of like a big scoop that had a draper to carry the seed in to be threshed, and we would have to grease all the inner parts of the machine before heading out to the field. There was a certain grease cup that was hard for my brother to reach. I'm a pretty small person, so one evening Bud got the bright idea of putting me *inside* the harvester, so I could reach the grease cup and keep everything greased down. So from sunup almost to sundown, I would have itchy clover seed chaff all over me. It wasn't very pleasant.

About four o'clock in the evening, it would be time to get the cows in to milk. Bud would ask me, "Pat, you want to keep harvesting, or would you like to get the cows in?"

"I'll go get the cows!" I'd cry. I was desperate to get away from the chaff I'd been breathing in all day. Getting the cows in to milk was a much better plan, and I would be looking forward and was most of all glad for a bath in the evening!

After the war ended, my brother Earl came home and helped with the harvesting. He had always been something of an inventor, and he put together a large vacuum that could be towed behind the tractor to suck up much of the clover seed that had been threshed out by the harvester. He also invented a way to separate the clover seed from the dirt that would inevitably suck up into the vacuum as well.

To this day, at ninety-seven years of age, Earl is still an inventor. I talked with him the other day, and he was working on something.

I am not sorry that my life no longer includes working with clover seed.

Flying Away

"And I said, Oh, that I had wings like a dove!
For then would I fly away, and be at rest."

—Psalm 55:6

y elder brother Earl always loved to fly airplanes. My parents even sent him to aeronautical school in Los Angeles (another example of my parents' progressive thinking). During World War II, whenever Earl came home on leave from the Air Force, he always wanted to go flying. And he was always ready to take his baby sister with him whenever he did.

"Come on, Pat," he would say. "Let's rent a plane and go flying."

At the time, small propeller planes were available for rent at the local airfield in Chico, and I loved flying with my brother. He even told me he would teach me to fly if I bought gas for the plane. Of course I was still just a young child and did not have the money at the time to purchase the gasoline for the plane. But I was always ready to go with my big brother.

One day when he was home on furlough, we rented a plane and decided to fly up to Cedarville, near the ranch where we used to live, to visit relatives. We had to go over the Sierra Nevada mountain range, and he gained a lot of altitude. I think we were up somewhere around 25,000 feet to get over the range when we ran into some turbulence. The plane began to bounce around. We hit an air pocket, and all of a sudden, the plane just dropped. Because the plane lost lift, it dropped straight *down*. It was over nearly as quickly as it had started, but my heart leapt up so high in my chest it almost came up in my mouth.

Earl pointed at the altimeter and said, "We dropped over a thousand feet." It was terrifying, yet it didn't stop me from going with my brother!

Another time, we decided to fly from Chico to the ranch in Ord Bend, where my other brother Bud and his wife, Marge, were living in the big house we had painted and fixed up. After circling the ranch house to let them know we were there and would need a ride, we landed in a nearby alfalfa field. Ed, Bud's brother-in-law, was up from southern California, and we had a nice visit with the family.

When it was time to leave, Bud and Ed drove us back to the plane. On the type of small plane Earl has procured for the day, the wings attached to the sides of the plane near the doors. A metal brace helped hold up the wing, and we had to crawl around the brace to get through the cockpit door.

I climbed into the co-pilot's seat first, before Earl got into the plane. A panel of gauges were facing me, and of course I didn't know anything about them.

"Keep your foot on the brake," Earl told me. Standing outside the plane, he reached in front of me to set the throttle, an action I did not observe with care. I knew about the throttle on a car, but planes have a lot more buttons and gizmos than a car does. Then he went around to the front of the plane to turn the propeller over to start the engine. There wasn't a starter on planes in those days. You could start them only by turning the prop over, similar to cars that had a crank in front instead of a starter button or ignition.

The plane started quickly with a roar and lurched forward. It started up so fast Earl had to throw himself out of the way before the plane ran him over.

Startled, I had no idea what to do. The plane shot forward, eating up the field, and I could barely hear anything above the thunder of the engine. An airplane has the engine up front, and there is no muffler on it. Many pilots use earplugs, in order to preserve their hearing. The noise of the plane was staggering. The engine blocked out almost every other sound. Earl ran alongside the plane and shouted at me from just a few feet away, but I could barely hear what he was saying.

Just as I was panicking, certain I was going to take off without him and inevitable crash, Earl managed to do the impossible—he dove his body part way into the moving plane.

"Adjust the throttle!" he yelled, hanging on to the door.

"I don't know which one it is!" I yelled back and pushed every button I saw, hoping one of them was right.

I grabbed Earl's clothes and tried to drag him inside as Bud and Ed grabbed hold of the tail section, one on each side, and tried to slow the plane down, digging the heels of their boots into the dirt. But the plane was just picking up speed. Finally, running as fast as he could while leaning inside the cockpit, Earl managed to adjust the throttle. The plane slowed, then stopped.

Everyone involved in my almost-solo flight was pretty shook up. Later, Earl told me, "Oh, it wouldn't have taken off. Don't worry."

But I knew better!

We went flying again—but before we did, he showed me where the throttle was on the instrument panel, just in case.

Several years later, the same thing happened at the Chico airport when a pilot was starting his plane alone. He turned the prop over, and the plane jumped the wooden blocks in front of the tires. It started taxiing, and it actually took off without him. The plane gained altitude and finally crashed in some foothills about ten miles north of Chico. When I saw the story on television, I reminded Earl of what he had told me.

"You'll never be able to convince me that that plane wouldn't have taken off with me in it!" I said.

Even though I had a couple of scares, it didn't deter me from going with my big brother on later flights when he would come home on furlough.

The War Horses

We didn't live in Ord Bend for very long because Dad's health couldn't take the heat. Barely a year later, he bought a house in Paradise, a town about forty miles northeast. But he kept the ranch in Ord Bend for a time, and in the summer, we would drive back and forth. Dad and I spent a lot of time driving from Paradise to our ranch, and we also attended cattle auctions in Orland, where he bought milk cows. Most were Holsteins, but he'd get a few Jerseys and Guernseys, too. They have richer milk, which increases the butter fat content in the milk. Since we still didn't have electricity anywhere on the ranch, all the milking had to be done by hand.

After the end of World War II, the government disbanded mounted infantry troops for the United States Army, once known as the United States Calvary, because they went to using motorized jeeps. The government began selling off the surplus horses. Each horse had a brand on its neck next to the mane with a long ID (like a soldier's dog tags) number to identify it. All cavalry horses had their manes roached (the term for cutting the manes) off. My dad loved good deals, and so he bought three of the horses, two blacks and a bay, for about fifty dollars per head at an auction in Chico. That was a good price for a horse if it was worth something, but these weren't! Dad ended up selling them pretty quick because they weren't trained for ranch work. They were trained to run hard after the enemy, and we didn't have too many of those in Ord Bend.

My Dad and Uncle Bud

While we were living north of Chico in a town called Paradise (which is always an amusing thing to say), my great-aunt Georgie and uncle Bud lived just up the road from us. Uncle Bud was my dad's uncle, and he was dying. Dad went up there every day to be with him and check on him. I remember my dad coming home one day and saying, "Bud is getting really bad." He never called him *Uncle*. He was always just *Bud*. Shortly after that, Dad said they had called the Baptist minister to come and talk to Bud. That was all he said about it.

Years later, when my husband and I were married and living in Redding, I was praying, and I asked the Lord, "Did my dad get right with You? Did he really give his heart to You?"

That night, I went to sleep and had an amazing dream. I heard my dad's voice, and I saw him and my mother in their wedding picture. Mom was sitting in a rattan chair, and she was all dressed up. They had gotten married in Reno by a Methodist minister and had gone to get their picture taken afterward. My dad was standing behind her, and I heard him say, "I got saved when Bud died." Then I saw his hand reached out to my mother and said as he pointed at her, "And then she got saved."

I woke up with a start, saying, "Bud? My brother Bud?" Still half-asleep, I shouted, "Bud's not dead!"

My husband startled awake, saying, "What? What?"

70

It was just a dream. But as I thought about it and prayed about it, I realized, *Oh, Uncle Bud! Dad got saved when Uncle Bud got saved. When they called the Baptist minister in to speak to Uncle Bud. And then my mother got saved years later.* I knew in my heart that God had answered my question concerning their salvation.

The Nice Boy Named Bill

*D*ad eventually decided the distance between our home in Paradise and his ranch in Ord Bend wasn't worth the effort of traveling back and forth all the time. Dad got word from one of the neighbors near the ranch that there was a small empty house one country block from the ranch—however just like the ranch, it didn't have electricity either. He rented it, and there I was again, doing chores and, after it got dark, I was doing my home-work by lantern light. The inside of that house was boards that had never been painted, so everything in the house was dark.

Not long after that, a small ranch came up for sale just out-side the nearby town of Durham, to the south of Chico, so in the summer between my freshman and sophomore years of high school, Dad added another ranch to his "empire." He, Mother, and I moved into the small house on the Durham property. It was another fixer-upper, but we got to buy all new furniture and carpet in Sacramento, which was pretty fun.

I was happy about the move, even though it meant making new friends. There wasn't a high school in Paradise at the time, so during my freshman year, I attended the large high school in Chico. Durham High School was much smaller, which I appreciated. Also, in Paradise I didn't have many places where I could ride my horse, Sandy. The roads were pretty busy, but in Durham, I could ride along Stanford Lane, which had very little traffic, and then take Sandy along the railroad tracks. The train seldom came by, and it was a nice grassy area to ride in. I also knew Sandy loved to catch the milkweed that was growing along with the grass. Sometimes I would just stop riding and let her have the pleasure of nibbling on the succulent weeds.

At Durham High, I took a typing class. It was made up of girls mostly, but there were a few boys, and I noticed one boy in particular. He was handsome, blond, and blue-eyed, and I found out that his name was Bill Arnold. He was a fast typist—the teacher told me it was unusual for a boy to be that good at typing—and he was getting good grades on his papers. He and I became acquainted through the class, and we received similar scores on our typing tests.

Bill was four years older than I, but he was repeating his senior year because he'd discovered that the teachers at the private school he'd attended weren't state-certified. Consequently, he hadn't received any credit for his senior year. I noticed Bill right away, but thought he had taken up with another girl. I'd heard a rumor that he was going steady with someone.

One day, Bill didn't show up for our typing class until seconds before the bell rang. He walked in, his face drawn and pale, and slid into his chair just in time.

"What happened to you?" I asked.

"I was in an accident," he replied. He had been driving by some orchards, and a truck backed out right in front of him and hit his Oldsmobile, smashing the front fender front really bad. He managed to pull the fender off the car so he could still get to school. He was pale from shock but uninjured. He didn't have a lot of money, so he decided to put an old tractor fender on the car as a replacement to keep off mud or anything else the tire picked up. I was just glad he was okay. The tractor fender remained on the Oldsmobile for years.

A short time after the school year had started, I was home after classes and heard a car come up the driveway. I glanced out the window and recognized the two boys inside: Bill Arnold and Jimmy, another boy from school. I knew that Jimmy liked me, so it didn't take much for me to guess what they were doing there.

After a few minutes, a knock sounded at the door, and I was surprised to see Bill standing there instead of Jimmy. What was Bill doing on the front porch?

"Would you like to go out to the show with me this weekend?" he asked. (We didn't usually call them movies back then. They were shows.)

He caught me completely off guard. I thought to myself, *Wasn't he going steady with somebody else?* I found out later that it was all speculation and rumor. Bill had driven that other girl home because she'd needed a ride. She had been in his car that one time, and from that one time, she had started the rumor. Apparently, I wasn't the only one who thought Bill was handsome.

As Bill waited expectantly on my front porch, I looked at him funny for a moment or two, and then I replied, "I'll have to ask my mother." Silently, I thought to myself, *And I don't think she'll say yes.*

"Okay," he said.

Mother was in the kitchen fixing dinner, and I secretly hoped she would say no, because at that time, I still thought Bill was with another girl. But, to my great surprise, Mother said I could go. She came into the front room and I introduced her to Bill.

"He wants me to go to a show with him," I said.

That was my first date with the boy who would be my husband for fifty-five years. The funny part of this story is that Jimmy really was the one who intended to ask me out. I later learned that he didn't have a car, so Bill volunteered to take him to my house. When they arrived at my place, Jimmy backed out of asking me out right at my front door. So Bill said, "I'll ask her out, then." And he did.

Years and years later, long after we were married, Bill told me that one day in the school cafeteria, he had looked across the room to where I was eating with my girlfriends and thought to himself, *I am going to marry that girl.*

It really was the Lord who brought us together. Bill was a devout Christian, and I had accepted the Lord as a child, but I didn't really know too much about Him. Back in those days, you weren't supposed to marry a non-Christian girl who wore lipstick and went dancing, and I was quite fond of both. But God was the one who was writing the story of my life and, about a year later, Bill and I got engaged.

I was fourteen years old when Bill asked me to marry him.

Jesus and the Windmill

*W*hen Bill and I started dating, he took me to church with him every Sunday. His dad, Carl, was a preacher, so Bill was used to attending church, while my family wasn't. We hadn't found much time on the ranch for church-going. It had never been a priority. I didn't comprehend the beauty and simplicity of what God had done for me, and it showed.

One Sunday when church was over, Bill and I got into his 1936 black Oldsmobile with the strapped-on tractor fender, and Bill turned to me. "What is it you're not understanding?" he asked.

"The preacher keeps saying that I am a sinner, but I don't believe that I am," I replied. "I'm not a sinner."

Bill explained, "But the Bible says, 'All have sinned and come short of the glory of God.'" He was quoting Romans 8:10. As Bill spoke those words, it was as if a dark veil suddenly peeled off my spirit. It was God giving me understanding. I could literally see the veil come off me, and my spiritual eyes opened.

The next time we went to church, when the minister gave the altar call, I went forward. As I got to the altar, a girl I had met in high school asked me if I had come to give my heart to Jesus.

"Yes," I replied.

She told me to kneel down and pray, but I didn't know how to pray. So she said, "Well, I will pray, and you can repeat the words after me." We knelt together and prayed the salvation prayer.

As I said the words, I felt as though a two-thousand-pound weight slid off my shoulders. That heavy weight of sin was gone! I didn't even know I had been so burdened with sin, but I certainly knew when it was gone! From that day forward, I found I was no longer living in darkness. I was given a new life, which the Bible talks about in 1 Peter 2:9—"But ye are a chosen generation, a royal priesthood, an holy nation, a people of his own that ye should show forth the praises of him, who hath called you out of darkness into his marvelous light."

A few weeks after receiving Jesus, I was baptized at Bill's church in Chico. Before the minister baptized me, he said something I still remember all these years later: He referred to a time when he had seen me carrying a banner in a parade. The minister said, "Now you are carrying the banner of the Lord." He also said, "Now that you know Jesus, He will answer your prayers."

Soon after that—I remember the exact date, it was May 19, 1947—my dad sent me out on his John Deere tractor to mow the alfalfa field. He had forgotten to give me a canteen, and it was a typical Sacramento Valley summer day—hot, dusty, and miserably dry.

I kept glancing at this old windmill standing at the edge of the field. When there was a wind, the blades on the windmill would start to turn and the attached pump drew water up from the well. We now use windmills as a natural energy source to turn turbines and create electricity. We no longer depend on these age-old devices to produce water from underground sources as we did when I was growing up.

But on that day, the windmill blades were at a standstill. It was very hot out, and there wasn't a breath of wind.

I remembered what the minister had said—that God would answer my prayers. So I prayed, "Lord, send some wind for this windmill." Sliding off the tractor, I released a wooden hand brake that prevented the windmill from turning when it wasn't being used to pump water for any livestock in the field.

I got back on the tractor and continued mowing the hay, keeping an eye on the windmill to see if it was turning. As I got farther away to the end of the field, I looked back and saw that the windmill was turning. I was so excited—I knew God had answered my prayer!

I quickly made my way to the windmill, and sure enough, water was pouring from the pump spout, even though I hadn't primed it. It pumped water into the trough for a long time. God had given me what I needed. I left the windmill going because I was so excited, and at each turn around the field, I would stop for a drink.

That was the first prayer I remember God answering. He has answered thousands of prayers since then, and He still is answering my prayers more than seventy years later.

The Wedding

*B*ill and I went together for several months. On January 26, 1947, on the way home from a movie, he asked me to marry him. I said yes.

On a Sunday morning soon afterward, Bill brought me home from church and got up his courage to ask my dad for permission to marry me. This etiquette was very unusual in my family. My brother Bud and sister Jean had both run off with their fiancés to Reno to get married without telling anyone. In our circle of family and friends, nobody ever got married in a church. I don't remember a single church wedding during my childhood. It was fixed in my mind that everybody who got married went to Reno to do it.

My parents liked Bill but they didn't know him very well. In some ways, our families were from two completely different worlds. My dad was in the Masonic Lodge and my mother was a member of the Order of the Eastern Star—a different Masonic organization. They always had doctors, dentists, and well-to-do people over for meals, hunting trips, and different events. We had some money because, as I said before, God had spared our finances in the 1929 stock market crash. This put us in a different category than some folks. Bill was from a family that wasn't as well-to-do, and I experienced some culture shock after we got married. Living with him on his parents' ranch wasn't the same as living with my folks.

I think my parents allowed me to marry him despite my young age because I was the only one in the family who would have a church wedding. They would be able to see a child get married, and it would be a special event to have the family involved. I know the Lord was involved as well, because it wasn't too much later when He spoke to me about my calling.

I decided on an informal wedding that would take place right after the morning service on November 9, 1947, in Chico. As Dad, Mother, and I were driving to the church that day, I told my dad, "Hurry up! You're driving very slowly!"

"Oh, it's okay," he teased. "They won't start without you." He was always teasing me and other folks.

During the morning service, the pastor informed the congregation that if they'd like to stay for our wedding, they were all invited. The church was already decorated for the ceremony, and most of the congregation stayed to attend.

As the shift was made from the regular service to the wedding, my sister, Jean, went up to play the piano. At the time, she and I had very similar features, and people often mistook the two of us. Later on, I was told that several people in the congregation thought I was playing the piano for my own wedding. Wouldn't that have been a trick?

Bill and I had made arrangements with the pastor to slip out a side door after the ceremony. We didn't want to get caught in the trap we suspected was being set for us. Bill was nineteen, and I was fifteen—we had many mischievous friends, and they liked "doing a cheuvre" after a wedding, where they grabbed the bride out of the getaway vehicle and carried her off. They were expecting us to leave in Bill's car, which he had left in an obvious spot in the church parking lot. They were all prepared to follow us out the main aisle and then out the front door, but we were sneaky. My brother-in-law, Jean's husband, had parked his pickup at the back of the church in the alley so we could make our escape. It was exciting, to say the least, trying to get out and get away.

The reception was at the ranch where my brother and sister-in-law lived on the other side of the Sacramento River. A ferry crossed the river at Ord Bend, but when we arrived, it was still on the other side, and we had to wait for it to come back over to our side of the bank.

As we were waiting for the ferry, the mischievous boys caught up with us. I hadn't thought about locking my truck door, so I was quite surprised when one of them opened my door and grabbed me. He tried to pull me out of the pickup, but thankfully by that time, other people from the wedding had begun to arrive, and they made the boys leave us alone.

We drove on to the ferry, and the ferryman pulled away from the banks so we would have the crossing to ourselves. After the reception, we left for a weeklong honeymoon along the California coastline and then returned to begin married life.

Married Life on the Arnold Ranch

*B*ill's uncle owned a ranch outside of Chico next to the Sacramento River where the water table was very high, and his parents lived and worked it under a rental agreement. His uncle was a well-to-do businessman who owned multiple butcher shops in San Jose, and he had purchased the ranch so Carl, Bill's father, could run it for him.

Bill's family lived in the main house while Bill and I started out in a small trailer. It had sinks but no toilets, so we had to pop into his parents' house to use the bathroom. They raised alfalfa and, later on, sugar beets.

We would all eat together in the evenings. His family liked me, but I think his little sister was concerned for my soul because I wore lipstick. One time when Bill and I were still dating, she came into the room where I was putting on lipstick in front of the mirror, and she informed me primly, "You're going to go to Hell!" Like many other women in that day, she was certain lipstick was a tool of God's enemy.

I looked at her and cockily replied, "Oh, really?" I hadn't been saved very long, but I knew she was mistaken.

My new life came with a new start, thanks to my earnings during the war. My dad helped me buy some cows by helping me cash in the war bonds that I had purchased while still in school during WWII, with the idea that my husband and I could start a dairy on the Arnold ranch.

After milking our cows in the early morning, I would jump on my horse and drive them out to pasture in the alfalfa fields after the fields had been mowed for the crop. There weren't any fences, but they could graze in the area, rest beneath the trees, and there was plenty of water for them to drink.

Afterward I would return to the barn and clean all the milking equipment and the milk room, where we cooled the milk from the machines and put it into ten-gallon cans. Each morning, the milk truck would come and pick up the milk to take it to the milk plant. I would do other chores throughout the day and help around the ranch. Then about 3:30 p.m., I would go back for the cows and bring them to the barn for the evening milking.

The cows had problems with flies and mosquitoes, and they would do whatever they could to get the pests away. One day, while I was driving them on horseback toward the barn, they had a problem much bigger than flies.

I was heading the cows home for the evening milking, driving them down the lane. There were bushes on both sides of the road, and I didn't realize there was a huge, cone-shaped hornets' nest almost a foot long hidden in the green leaves. As the cows went by, they rubbed up against the bushes to get rid of the flies and mosquitoes. All of a sudden, a large swarm of hornets came rushing out of the bushes and attacked the cows. I was definitely not created to be a hero. I took off charging past the cows to the barn. The cows started bawling and followed me—they didn't want to get stung either. The next time I drove them for the milking, I took the cows home a different way.

The Ornery Pet Pig

ill's dad raised hogs, and one evening a large sow went into labor. She was so big that Carl, my father-in-law, was concerned she would crush the piglets during birth. The litter was huge—somewhere around twelve or fifteen—and as the lighting was pretty poor in the barn, we watched her with flashlights and snatched the piglets out of the way as each one came.

By the time she was finished, the hour was late, and it was pretty dark outside. Carl thought we should take two of the piglets into the house because there were so many of them. He didn't want to lose any. Also, they were the runts, or smallest ones.

So Bill and I each took a piglet, and for people who might not know, little pigs squeal loud and long when they are picked up. The sow was grunting and squealing. The piglets were squealing. The night was filled with the ruckus. Bill and I started jogging toward the house, each of us with a squealing pig in hand in the dark. He was right behind me, and I don't know why, but I got spooked. I started imagining an angry mother sow chasing us because we'd stolen her babies, so I took off. I ran for the house and slammed the door in Bill's face.

"Let me in! Let me in!" he shouted.

"Oh, it's you," I said, relieved.

The next day, we returned just one of the piglets to his mother, and we kept the other to raise by hand. For a time, we fed him from a bottle with a nipple on it. He was such a cute little pig. He was black with orange stripes going down his back, sort of like a zebra. When he was three or four months old, he was about the size of a large puppy, and we let him run loose around the barn and the outside of the corral. He made a nice pet, and at that point, he hadn't gotten into any trouble. We called him "Pig," and he was certain I was his mama. I remember hanging clothes out on the line, and he would come up and root on my leg with his snout so hard that it almost made my leg sore. He would do that to Bill also when he was working on equipment out in the barn area.

One evening, Bill and I were milking the cows in the barn. We had a milking machine by this point, but Carl always milked one certain cow by hand because her milk had more cream in it than the others.' She was a Jersey, a breed that produces richer milk, and he wanted to keep it separate.

I left for a few minutes, and when I returned, it was just in time to see Pig darting underneath Carl's special cow. He was sitting on a milk stool on the cow's right side, so he didn't see him. That little pig had his eye on the milk bucket, and he jumped into it headfirst! Startled, the cow kicked the bucket and knocked Carl over into the manure trough. Milk went all over the floor and all over Carl. Pig wanted that bucket, and the only way Carl could get him out of it was to grab him by the ears and pull.

Dripping milk and manure, he shouted at Bill and me, "KEEP THAT PIG OUT OF THIS BARN!"

We did just that. After the incident with the cow, Pig stayed penned up during milking.

A Harrowing Narrow Escape

*T*he summer after Bill and I got married, three of us—Bill, Carl, and I—were out in the sugar beet field, digging an irrigation ditch. Bill and Carl didn't really need me, but I didn't want to go back and just sit in the house. Carl was driving the tractor, and half the time, he was turned around in the seat looking at Bill, who was making the ditch with an implement called, remarkably, a ditcher. I was riding on the harrower attached to the front of the tractor, just to have something to do.

As we were going along the fence line, we came to a bent iron fence post, but nobody saw it. The harrower caught that iron post, and I saw it twist around like a metal hand that almost seemed alive. It somehow pushed me off the top of it and dropped me on my face in front of the tractor. Before I could move, the harrower went over the top of me and ripped up the seat of my jeans. I was screaming, but no one could hear me above the roar of the tractor and other equipment noise. I couldn't lift my head because the harrower was right there on top of me.

There are times in life when something happens, and when all is said and done, you know God saved you. The big rear wheel of the tractor got within five inches or less of my feet. It would have traveled up my entire body and crushed me, but Carl just happened to turn around in time to see me beneath the harrower. He grabbed the clutch and stopped the tractor.

I was pretty shaken up. "I am sure glad you heard me scream," I told him.

"I didn't hear you," he replied. "I just turned around and saw you lying underneath the machine."

I'm just very grateful God hears the cries of His children, because no one else did that day.

The Naming of Linda Kay

*B*ill and I lived in the little trailer on his family's ranch for about a year. Then they had to move off the ranch into town because his mother had developed some bad physical problems. She went into a diabetic coma and ended up having a stroke. The ranch was twenty miles outside of town, and they just couldn't stay there anymore due to her medical needs.

We sold our cows and headed into Chico. Bill and I purchased a house, and he kept working on ranches. He would plant crops and help with the haying until the rains came and the ranch work ended; then he would find odd jobs in town. For a while, he worked in a used car lot, washing the cars and repairing them.

Before we moved off his parents' ranch, I started to really want a baby. The desire got to be overwhelming, and I realized it was something the Lord was doing in my heart. I had always wanted to have kids—but not any boys. My brother and sister both had boys, and, in my perception, they were both little terrors. I only wanted girls.

When I found out I was pregnant, I was very excited. We had fun fixing up a room in our new house for the baby. In the 1940s, there was no way of knowing whether you were having a boy or a girl, so I talked to God about it and prayed, hoping for a girl.

This was before the advent of television, and I had been listening to *Art Linkletter's House Party* on the radio. Art always interviewed five

88

first- and second-graders on his program, and one day, he asked one of the little girls, "What is your name?"

"Linda Kay," she replied in a precious little voice.

It was so cute that when Bill got home from work, I told him I liked that name for the baby. He didn't have any ideas or opinions about baby names, so I was able to name the baby anything I wanted.

"Sounds good to me," he said.

The baby was two weeks late, and the doctor told me to get a five-ounce bottle of castor oil at the drugstore. This was common practice in our day for women who wanted to induce labor if one thought it was past time. (I'm not recommending it for other women, just telling what we used to do during those days.) I mixed it with orange juice to get it down, and my labor started soon afterward. Twenty-seven hours later, our eight-pound, ten-and-a-half-ounce baby girl arrived. We named her Linda Kay.

Three years later in the same month, our daughter Penny Raye was born in Westwood, thirteen miles east of Chester. I had two baby girls born in June. It was the answer to my heart's desire for girls. God always knows the desire of our hearts and, if it is in line with His plan, we are blessed with those desires. To know His will is to read His Word and pray for guidance by His will.

The Chester Saga

*W*e eventually moved to Chester, up in the Northern California mountains, so Bill could get full-time work. On a ranch in that area it isn't always practical to work year-round due to the weather, and we'd heard that a sawmill in Chester was looking for full-time help. Bill was always a hard worker, and it was easy for him to find a job.

The winter I was expecting Penny, Chester and the surrounding area had seventeen feet of snow on the level. It wasn't seventeen-foot drifts—it was actually seventeen feet straight down everywhere. It snowed night and day for a week and a half or more. It just kept coming.

Bill and I were home alone. It so happened that the week before the record snowfall, we had gone down to my mother's in Durham, and she asked if Linda could stay with her. My dad had passed away when Linda Kay was three months old. Scarlet fever had enlarged his heart, which the doctors didn't discover until after he'd had several heart attacks. After his death, Mother stayed in Durham, the small town where I had met Bill.

So he and I were alone when the big snow came, which was good. It would have been difficult to have a two-hand-a-half-year-old trapped indoors with us. Linda was a rambunctious child. An aunt once told her that she looked like a little spider because she was always so busy and, like a spider, she could run so fast when you tried to get her. Linda was always very quick.

None of the buildings in Chester had ever seen that much snow before, and the company that owned the mill was afraid the roofs would collapse. The bosses were concerned for the storage buildings, for the lumber, and the mill building itself, due to the snow loads. The workers heated up water from the millpond and used steam hoses under the roofs, inside the buildings, which warmed the roofs and caused the snow to melt. Then other men would climb on top of the buildings with push brooms and shove the snow off. They had to be careful because the layers of snow were three to four feet deep, sometimes they'd let loose in a miniature avalanche.

Each day when Bill got home from work, I would be sitting in the dark because the storm had knocked out our electricity. All of our kitchen appliances were electric, so we made good use of candles and the oil stove. Fortunately, the week before the storm, we'd had the oil truck come out and fill up our oil tank, so at least we had heat. I would take the grate off the stovetop and melt buckets of snow, which gave us water to drink and to use in the toilets. I learned that it takes a lot of snow to make a gallon of water. I was about six months pregnant with Baby Number Two, and that didn't help matters either.

It was snowing so hard that from one day to the next, more than three feet of snow piled on the roof. The house started to creak and crack and groan from the snow's weight. I would listen to the house shift and feel a little nervous. Every day when Bill came home from a hard day of taking care of the snow at the sawmill, he would have to shovel off his own roof.

Snow enveloped the whole house. The windows were completely covered up, and during the day, all you could see was a bluish-white hue. You could get some light, but it wasn't all that bright.

"Could you tunnel down to the windows so I could have some light?" I finally asked Bill. I was beginning to feel claustrophobic. I had seen nothing but bluish-white snow for days. He dug down to the windows so I could have real light.

From somewhere lower down the valley, they flew in supplies and the mail, and dropped them off by parachute. My doctor lived in Chester near the mill, and he got angry with the road crews because they were supposed to open up his driveway so he could get to the hospital seventeen miles away. He had to cancel an appointment with me because the road crew hadn't done his driveway, and he was going to have to shovel it by hand. Just imagine—heavy snowfall day and night for a week and a half! It might have been longer. It certainly seemed longer.

Bill and I lived only a block from the main road and about half a mile from the store. One day, he asked me if I wanted him to pull me on the toboggan up to the store because our food supply was starting to get pretty low. I hadn't been out of the house the entire time, and I was going stir crazy. So Bill got a rope and tied the toboggan around his waist. I managed to get my very pregnant self onto the toboggan, my feet on the curled prow.

As we got onto the main road, which had been plowed, a man came along in a pickup and asked if we would like him to tow us. We got to the store, only to discover that it was nearly empty. We found a few items and then headed back home.

Finally, after a week and a half, maybe two, of continual snowfall, the sky quieted down, and the storm passed. The last time Bill climbed up onto the roof to shovel, he actually had to toss each shovelful upward because the piles around the house had gotten so tall.

Our friends who had moved up with us from Chico said, "As soon as spring comes, we're getting out of this country." Bill and I said we were leaving as soon as the baby was born.

When the mountain roads opened up, we were finally able to go down to pick up Linda from my mother.

It had stopped snowing, but we were left with mountains of white everywhere. The weather remained cold, and the snow didn't melt, and months passed before we saw the ground again. I remember patches of snow in our yard all the way through May. I got so weary of seeing snow. I went out with a shovel and tried to break the snow into chunks, hoping that might cause it to melt more quickly.

We moved from Chester back to Chico as soon as Penny was born in June. Nowadays, I get excited when I see a little bit of snow, but I never want to relive that record snowfall of 1952. It is so amusing to me when I hear on the news of an area having a few inches of snow—they don't know what snowfall is. Seventeen feet of snow on the level is a whole different kind of news story. I lived it, and all of it is true.

Chester, California 1952, record snowfall.

The Joys of False Labor

When I was pregnant with Penny Raye, I had false labor on and off for an entire month. It was so deceiving that I went to the hospital seventeen miles away in Westwood and spent the entire night in labor, pains coming three to five minutes apart. The doctor thought that the baby might be breaching and decided to take an X-ray to be sure. As it turned out, the baby was not breach, but by the time we discovered that, the contractions had stopped. There was nothing to do but go home. My sweet little Penny Raye didn't decide to make her appearance for three more weeks!

I kept saying, "If I have to go to the hospital and come back again, I'm going to have this baby in the car first." It was embarrassing. It was my second baby—I should have known real labor from false, but it kept happening. My daughter Linda was at my mother's in Durham for almost the entire last month of my pregnancy because I had so many false starts.

Finally, I began to have contractions every three to five minutes, and this time, I knew it was real labor. When Bill came home from work, I told him it was time to go. We didn't have a phone, so we had to stop by the doctor's house on the way.

"Are you sure this time?" the doctor asked.

"Oh, yes," I replied. "I am sure." There were other more obvious signs of the real thing.

Bill and I continued on to the hospital, but before we got out of Chester, he suddenly turned to me and asked, "Do you think I've got time to get a haircut?" He still wasn't quite certain my labor was real yet.

I looked at him in surprise. "Well, I don't know," I answered slowly, "but if you can park right in front of the barber shop, then maybe you do..." *You crazy man*, I thought to myself.

The old barber in that one-horse town was like a lot of other old barbers—he would visit and talk with his customers. Getting your hair cut could take a while. When he had a customer, he would close the blinds and then settle in for a long chat. I wanted Bill to park in front so I could see him through the window and let him know if he needed to run out.

"Don't let that barber close those venetian blinds!" I ordered.

Well, after about fifteen minutes, that barber went over and closed the blinds, and I lost sight of Bill. I don't think he ever told the barber that his wife was in the car about to give birth. The contractions got stronger and stronger, and I was afraid that if I got out of the car and tried to walk into the shop, my water would break. I didn't think I could make it to the door.

Bill, oblivious to my plight, finished his haircut. He was having a nice visit with the barber and didn't come out for an hour.

"Get over to the hospital quick," I said, gasping, when he finally returned. "Get going. You'd better hurry."

I think it was about thirteen miles from Chester to the hospital in Westwood. We'd traveled those miles several times in the last month, and this time, it seemed to take forever. By the time we arrived, it was getting dark, and I was right on the threshold of giving birth in the car. Yes, and even bring to pass the very words I had said almost a month earlier: "I'll have this baby in the car before I have to come home without having the baby."

This is where the story gets interesting. Let me describe the well-thought-out, pleasantly planned delivery room of this hospital. It was on the second floor. There were no elevators. There were no regular stairs. To get to the delivery room, you had to climb up the wall via something that could only be described as a glorified ladder. I think there was a rail on one side, but it wasn't a lot of help. I was big and pregnant, about to give birth at any moment—and they expected me to climb a ladder. The steps were steep, and Bill had to come behind me and push. Each time a contraction hit, all I could do was grab my belly, which was getting lower and lower with each step, and hold to the rail for dear life. We finally reached the delivery room.

Five babies had been born in that room that night, and they had to clear the room for me; the baby born right before mine was still there. There was only one birthing table and only one basket for the newborn.

They dressed me in a hospital gown, and the doctor ordered a pain shot.

"I'm going to give you this because the doctor ordered it," the nurse told me. "But you're not going to need it. When the next contraction hits, I want you to push hard."

She leaned over me, and when the next contraction came, I pushed as she'd instructed. My water broke and splashed all over her uniform.

"I'm so sorry!" I said, mortified.

"Nonsense, honey," she replied. "It's happened before."

A short time later, I gave birth to an eight-and-a-half-pound baby girl.

It was quite the day for Bill. He had a new daughter *and* a new haircut. How proud and happy could one man be?

God's Call

We attended a little church in Chester called Chester Assembly of God, and we got to know the pastor and his wife. They were really sweet people who wanted to know God well. They didn't want to know Him from a distance; they wanted real relationship with Him.

One of my close girlfriends and I both wanted a closer walk with the Lord and decided to go to church and pray every afternoon. We did this for several weeks as the extreme hunger for more of God came over us. During one of these prayer times, I suddenly heard God speak to me.

I don't know whether it was audible—but it was so clear in my right ear. He asked me, "Will you preach My Word?"

Immediately, I asked in my heart and I said back to Him, *How can I?* I had been a Christian for only a few years, and I didn't have much knowledge of the Bible. I was just learning what the voice of God sounded like.

But God had plans. After I asked that question, my friend stopped praying. She said, "The Lord is able to do that what He would have you to do."

I hadn't said anything aloud about my short conversation with God, and I knew He was using her to answer my question. He was letting me know that preaching His Word didn't depend on me and my abilities—it was up to Him, because He had called me. Over the years, God has been faithful to do exactly what He said He would do. I have so many stories of His faithfulness to fulfill what He said in reply to my question, "Lord how can I?"

The Great Salmon Caper

a short time after Penny was born, we moved back to Chico, into the same house we had lived in before moving to Chester. The people who owned the house were friends of ours and lived right next door.

Bill had an offer from a rancher to come and work for him, but before he did that, he heard about work at the fish hatchery in Cottonwood, where they needed men to separate the roe from the fish for the hatching process. Rather than pay the men in money, they paid them in salmon. We had a 1946 Dodge coupe with a humongous trunk, and they filled the trunk to overflowing with fish. They had trouble shutting the trunk door because there were so many salmon, and they were slick. Bill had to slam the door fast.

We didn't have a fence around our back lawn in Chico where we lived, so Bill drove behind the house, and when he opened up the trunk, some of the fish popped out and slithered onto the grass. Back then, as we still have today, we could rent a frozen storage unit called an ice locker from butchering companies. We contacted a vendor with an ice locker and said we needed to rent one. We explained our salmon dilemma to the vendor and said we needed butcher paper to wrap all the salmon in. We let them know it probably would take quite a long time to get this all done.

The four of us—our neighbor and his wife, and Bill and I—started a salmon-cleaning assembly line on the back porch. We had a double wash tray, and we cleaned up the fish, gutted them, cut them into large chunks, and then wrapped them in butcher paper. We filled boxes and laundry baskets with packages of fish and took them down to the ice locker, where we had rented a freezer the way you would a storage unit. It was probably eleven or twelve o'clock by the time we finished.

Even though getting large quantities of meat for the winter was our way of life, I got so sick of eating salmon. For a while, I didn't care if I ever ate it again! We had to get very creative in the ways we used it. Bill's father bought us a big gunnysack of red beans, and between the salmon and the beans, we had food that lasted through the winter. We didn't have a lot of money at the time, but that didn't matter—we had salmon and beans. Back then the most important thing was having enough to get through the winter and coming up with inventive ways to create variety, whether when preparing the food for storage or cooking with different seasonings and spices.

Linda was about three at that time, and one day, I noticed she kept picking her nose.

"Linda, stop that," I'd say, and then a few minutes later, I'd look over and she'd be doing it again.

Finally, I got a Kleenex and helped her blow her nose. "Blow," I commanded. And then: "Blow harder."

She blew hard, and out came a bean. That legume had lodged in her nasal cavity and sprouted! The last time I'd cooked with beans had been about a week before, and I couldn't believe it. When Bill got home, I told him what had happened and showed him the bean that had sprouted in our daughter's head. Children can get into, and survive, the most amazing situations.

The Popsicle
and the Truth

*M*y daughters have always had minds of their own, even when they were little, but truth always prevails.

One Sunday morning at church when Linda was about five, I was sitting in the back of the room waiting for her to return from Sunday school. In between the church and the small Sunday school building was a mom-and-pop grocery store. Right about the time Sunday school was over, I just happened to look through the door and spied Linda and one of her little girlfriends step into the church foyer.

I couldn't believe what I saw. Instead of putting their Sunday school money in the offering, they had gone to the store and bought popsicles. But they hadn't planned their escapade very well, for apparently, they had purchased the popsicles before the class and kept them to eat afterward. It was really hot that day, and the popsicles were melting in rivers. Pink liquid ran down their arms.

I dashed over to Linda and her friend and got them into the restroom. "You girls stay here," I said, and told her little friend, "I'm going to go find your mom." It's funny now, but at the time, I was horrified—my child covered in popsicle juice at church. The popsicles had melted so badly that the girls couldn't even eat them anymore.

A few weeks later, Linda started school. Her little elementary school was only about four blocks away from our house in Chico.

I drove her to school the first morning, but the second morning, I saw her all ready to go and headed toward the door.

"Now, Linda," I said, "just a minute. I'll get the car."

She replied lightly, "No, I'll walk," and she started off.

"Oh," I said, trying not to laugh. "It's quite a ways. You don't really know where it is."

"I know where it is," she answered. She was just this tiny little thing, and she was so confident, it was funny.

"Well, are you sure?" I called after her because by this time, she was halfway down the block.

"Yes, I can walk. It's only right up the road," she replied.

So I let her walk, but I followed her, just to make sure she got there safely, just as my mother did with me that day I wanted to follow my brother to the post office on my tricycle. When I saw that Linda was capable, the next day, I let her walk to school on her own.

The sad truth of the world today is we can't allow children to confidently learn about the world around them and grow up without being cautious and careful, as we could in that more innocent time.

The New Job, the Old Man and the Angel

When Linda and Penny were both still very little, Bill had an offer from Mr. Carter, the boss of a 9,000-acre ranch outside of Chico. Bill had been working for the ranch off and on during the summer months. They would call him when they needed extra hands. Mr. Carter liked Bill's work, so when he needed a man to run the rice dryer, Mr. Carter came to our door and asked Bill if he'd like to come work steady, which would be good for us. In addition, the job came with a house on the property, so we would no longer have to pay rent. Mr. Carter was called "the old man," because his son worked on the ranch as well.

So the four of us moved onto the ranch. When he wasn't in the dryer, Bill spent most of his time at the office, where the trucks filled with freshly harvested rice would drive onto the scale to be weighed. Then they would drop off their loads into a deep pit in the floor, and conveyor belts took it to clean out the straw and go on to the process of drying the newly harvested rice.

One time, when Penny was about four years old, she was outside playing and saw Mr. Carter. He had just pulled up and was climbing out of his car. She went running into the office, shouting, "The old man's here." I just cringed because I was embarrassed.

Mr. Carter heard her and started laughing. He was used to having people call him the old man, but not our little Penny. She had picked up the name from hearing other people say it.

FROM RANCH TO ROYALTY

During that period of time, I was helping a woman in town who was very ill with cancer. I felt the Lord wanted me to help her through this very difficult time, and I was praying for confirmation. One night while I was sleeping, I had a spiritual experience that confirmed in my heart I was doing this work for the Lord and not myself.

Around two o'clock in the morning, a whooshing noise suddenly interrupted my sleep. A gust of wind blew my bangs off my forehead, and I awoke with a start. Immediately, I knew some kind of presence was in the room with me. I didn't have to really think about it—I knew it was an angel. It really startled me.

What are you supposed to do when you realize there's a presence you can't see in your bedroom? I got out of bed and went to pray. "God, what is this? What do You want?" He didn't say anything to me that night, but I believed at the time, and still do, the Lord was giving me comfort and confirmation that I was walking the path He wanted me to and doing His will by caring for the woman in town.

God's Clear Answer

*A*fter accepting Christ, I firmly believed I was supposed to be a preacher. Before our kids were born, I had been voted in as the youth group leader in our Assemblies of God church in Chico. I didn't play any instruments, but I led the singing while other group members played. That was how I cut my spiritual teeth—by leading worship. The pastors encouraged me, and two of them in particular were extremely supportive as I grew in my leadership abilities. But I still had questions.

One day, I was outside hanging clothes out to dry, and I asked the Lord, "Have You really called me to preach?" I knew what He had whispered in my ear up in Chester, when I was praying with my friend at church. but He hadn't said anything more. I felt it was pretty clear that God had called me to preach, but the Bible says that out of the mouths of two or three witnesses a thing will be established (Deuteronomy 19:15), so I was waiting for confirmation.

The pastor at the Pleasant Valley Assembly of God called to tell me about a special meeting at their church. "You should try to come if you can," she said. Pleasant Valley was on the other side of town, about four miles away. She knew about some physical problems I had been having and I was praying that God would touch and heal me.

I have struggled with physical ailments for many years, and the Lord has always been with me throughout those trials. Prior to that invitation, for about five years, I had been getting one-sided headaches, where I would feel intense pain behind my right ear. My reflexes on one side of my body were diminished. I had gone through a lot of very intense and difficult tests to find out what was happening, and the doctors were afraid I had a brain tumor. They had prescribed medication that contained aspirin to help control the pain, but it gave me ulcers, and I had to have two surgeries, the last of which removed most of my stomach.

In those years, we didn't have technology like CAT scans and MRIs, and the tests we did have were pretty vague, but I knew the protein levels in my spinal fluid were elevated.

I wanted to go to the Pleasant Valley meeting, even though I was having the physical problems.

"I'll try to make it," I told the pastor. I already had plans that evening, so I told her I might come a little late.

"That would be fine," she said.

By the time I got to the church, the service was over. The minister put a chair in the middle of the room and said that when I was ready for prayer, I could go ahead and sit down. As I sat in the chair, he asked me, "Are you going to mind the Lord?"

The question took me by surprise. "Yes," I said. I thought I had been obeying the Lord, but the minister kept repeating the question. He said it so many times that it almost began to make me angry. At last, I said firmly, "Yes."

He then began to pray for me and prophetically said the exact words God had spoken to me in Chester through my friend and prayer partner: "Haven't I said to you that the Lord is able to do what He would have you to do?" This answer took the pressure off me and put it on the Lord.

That night at the meeting in church, God confirmed what He wanted me to do with my life, and He began to arrange for me to be a leader. As opportunity arose, I took Bible study courses, led worship, and preached on occasion. Our family started attending

Faith Tabernacle Assembly Church in Redding, and the pastor asked me to preach and lead worship regularly on Sunday evenings.

We lived a very long distance from the church and, often as I was making the drive, I would start to sense that I would be leading worship that night, though the pastor hadn't said anything to me about it. So, keeping a hand on the steering wheel, I would write down the choruses and songs of worship as I drove to the church.

And sure enough, the pastor would be standing at the church door when I arrived. "Sister Arnold, would you lead worship tonight?" he'd ask.

"Yes, I'm all ready," I'd reply.

When the pastor discovered that a number of people in his congregation were called to preach, he invited the overseer of the denomination to come up and ordain us through the church organization, which meant that we could legally officiate at weddings and funerals, and perform other pastoral duties.

The journey of following God is full of ups and downs, mistakes and victories ... but that is the life of the faithful and obedient. He is my sweet Lord, and He keeps His word and has never failed me.

The Gray Mare from Crazy Town

Bill and I took a trip to Las Vegas to visit Bill's Uncle Arthur and Aunt Lynn. In his younger days, Uncle Arthur had toured with Buffalo Bill in Wild West shows as a trick rider, doing rope tricks and other things. Even years later, he would always greet everyone with a handshake and a "Hellooo, Cowboy!"

In their younger days, Uncle Arthur and Aunt Lynn had owned thousands of acres outside Las Vegas, and eventually they sold it to the government, which used the land as the range where they tested the atomic bomb—most people know it now as Area 51. I'm sure Arthur received a lot of money for his property, but he was a down-to-earth old cowboy, and you'd never know he was wealthy.

When Bill and I visited them, they were caretakers of a non-working dude ranch north of Las Vegas. The ranch was fully equipped with everything a dude ranch needed: a large herd of horses for trail rides, an Olympic-sized swimming pool, and a dozen guesthouses. I still think fondly about that pool. Bill and I picked a guesthouse right next to the pool and swam late into the night, every night.

A few days into the trip, I asked Uncle Arthur if Bill and I could choose a couple of horses and ride over to a small mountain range I had seen off to the east. My eyes roamed over the horses in the corral, and I immediately saw a gray mare I wanted to ride. I picked her simply because I'd never ridden a gray before. I asked

Uncle Arthur about the mare, and he said she was pretty spunky, but he knew I'd been riding and breaking horses from an early age.

"You can handle her," he said.

"What do you use for a bridle?" I asked.

"A hackamore," he replied.

That should have been a clue right there. A hackamore is a headstall fashioned from braided rawhide that goes over the horse's nose and ears and is buckled around the jaw. It's similar to a halter in that there isn't a bit in the mouth—it works by exerting pressure on the nose. With a hackamore, you don't quite have as good control of the horse. Bill, wise man that he was, decided to ride a sorrel gelding that was very quiet.

We saddled up and rode toward the mountain range; I hadn't been horseback riding in some time. It was a lot of fun. We walked the horses for a while, but eventually, I told Bill, "Let's gallop. It's a long way to that mountain range."

As I kicked my horse into a gallop, she put her head down and started bucking. I hadn't been expecting her to go into rodeo mode, and I couldn't get her to settle down. She threw me, and I landed on my back right beneath her—just in time to see her hind legs drawn up toward her belly. I knew what was about to happen. I had been around horses enough to know that when the legs go up, they come down again.

But it was fine. The next thing I knew, I was out from under the horse. I got up and brushed myself off, amazed that I was all in one piece without any hoof imprints on my face. My horse was still going crazy, throwing herself sideways and bucking off into the sunset.

"Are you all right?" Bill asked, worried. "I don't know how you weren't trampled."

I didn't understand why I wasn't trampled either, having seen horse behavior for my entire life. I had landed right under the horse lengthwise, looking into those drawn-up hind feet and legs. I had seen hooves coming straight toward my body. Then, all of a sudden, the horse didn't smash me into pieces.

"I'm fine," I said. "Go get my horse."

Bill raced after the mare and managed to bring her back. "You are not going to get back on her," he said.

"Oh, yes, I am. I'm going to ride her back," I said hotly. "I know how to ride her now. I'll walk her, and she won't buck."

It didn't make sense that I hadn't been trampled. Later, I realized that an angel must have pushed me out of harm's way because the Lord had His plans for me.

Because of that fool horse, we never made it to the mountains. We turned around and headed back for the ranch. It only confirmed for me that even a horse's natural inclination has to bow down to the Lord's will when His children need protection.

Heaven's Melody

*I*n 1953, due to physical problems, I needed an abdominal surgery. In those days, you were left in bed to recuperate, instead of getting up to walk and move around, as they do now. Three days after the surgery, the nurses helped me out of bed for the first time, and right away, we discovered something was wrong. I passed out.

They took my blood pressure and discovered it was so low it was almost nothing. I had lost nearly half of my blood volume and was now in critical condition. The doctor ordered blood work so he could find out what was wrong.

I broke out in a rash from head to toe, and my temperature spiked to around 103. Eventually, they realized what had happened—I had been given the wrong type of blood during the first transfusion. That night when Bill came to the hospital to see me, I was unable to speak, except to whisper, "Get someone to pray."

The doctor told me, "If this doesn't stop in a few hours, we are going to have to go in and open you back up to find where you are bleeding." I wasn't passing any of this blood so it was apparent that it was collecting internally.

I was near death at that point. My body was in bad shape, but my mind wasn't. I began to think about the glory and majesty of God. All through the night, I felt His presence strongly. It felt like ocean waves rolling through me. That's the only way I can explain it. Then, at some point in the night, I started to hear the music of Heaven—the praises of people and angels worshiping God. I believe I was so close to death that the veil between Earth and Heaven had thinned enough that I could hear the melody.

That night, the Lord healed me. The bleeding stopped, and after five or six transfusions, I didn't need additional surgery.

God's Hand of Protection

*E*ventually, we moved to Red Bluff, California, where Bill started a welding and car repair shop. One day, he was installing a trailer hitch on the back of a garbage truck. He was underneath the truck, welding with his helmet on, and after a while, he smelled gasoline and felt something wet coming down his sleeve. He pushed up his welding helmet to see a spreading pool of gasoline beside him. He was soaked with gasoline—with his welding torch still lit in his hand. Aware of the serious danger he was in, Bill quickly extinguished it.

He hadn't realized how close, or how full, the gas tank on the truck was. The gasoline had expanded from the torch's heat and was leaking out the tank's spout. Bill scooted out from underneath the truck, thanking God for His protection.

When he came home and told me about it, obviously, I was alarmed.

"Well, God's angel protected you," I exclaimed.

At that time, God's angel must have been pretty busy with the lot of us. In 1961, just a few months later, we were driving home from Chico after a special meeting. In the car were my husband, two daughters, and the guest speaker. It was just after midnight, and it was dark. We took a shortcut to get back to Red Bluff.

Penny was asleep on the seat next to me. Her head was on my lap with her feet on the floor. Linda and the speaker were both asleep in the back seat. Bill and I were the only ones awake. We were gathering speed on the little back road when suddenly, a car pulled out in front of us.

I tried to shout to Bill, "He is not going to stop!" but we hit him before the words came out.

It was a head-on collision. There weren't any seatbelt laws at the time, so there was nothing to restrain any of us. We were in a large, two-door Chrysler sedan, and the front seats collapsed forward, shoving me into the windshield with enough force that I nearly went through it. I blacked out momentarily.

When Bill opened his door, the dome light came on, and I saw that Penny had blood all over her face. She had a gash on her forehead from being thrown under the dashboard. The passenger in our car had been thrown up against the ceiling, and he'd hit his head pretty severely. He was in a bad way. Bill, Penny, and I climbed out of the car. Poor little Linda was in shock.

The accident had happened in front of several homes, and people came running out to make sure we were all right. One of the houses nearby belonged to a friend we knew from church. I walked around the back of the car, and she asked, "Pat? Is that you?"

It was so dark that we hadn't recognized each other, but when she told me her name, I knew who she was. "Yes, it's me. Can someone get a washcloth for Penny? Because she is bleeding badly." That was all I could think of. I needed a washcloth for my daughter.

When I tried to turn my head, horrible pain rushed up my neck, and I realized something was badly wrong with me. I put my hand on the top of my skull and felt shards of glass. Someone called the emergency services. Neither Bill nor Linda was injured, but Penny, the passenger, and I were transported to a hospital in Red Bluff.

I remember being X-rayed and given medication for the pain. To this day, I don't remember hitting the windshield. I found out later that I had a concussion.

A friend took Bill and Linda home. When they got out of the friend's car, Linda dropped the small chain belt she'd taken off and had been fiddling with in the car. The belt landed on the driveway, and as she went to pick up, she suddenly screamed and jumped back.

"What's the matter?" Bill asked.

"I thought it was a snake," she said.

"It's just your belt," he replied, realizing she was still in shock.

I was in the hospital for about two weeks in cervical traction, and when I finally was able to go home, I didn't get any better. I was in such excruciating pain that it made me nauseous and I would be violently sick and throw up.

My chiropractor referred me to a neurosurgeon in San Jose, who discovered I had two or three ruptured discs in my neck, and I needed to have surgery. In those days, they didn't use donor bones, so he removed a bone chip from my right hip and inserted it into in my cervical spine in my neck. It was a brand-new type of surgery at the time and almost experimental.

Shortly after the first surgery, Bill and I went for a walk around the block. I started having extreme pain in my lower spine, and it shot down my leg. I returned to San Jose for another myelogram, a special diagnostic test involving injecting dye into the spine. It was the same test they used for my upper cervical to diagnose the ruptured cervical discs in my neck. This time the neurosurgeon found a ruptured disk in my lumbar (lower) spine that had caused the cushioning to fail between the vertebrae. Once more, I needed serious spinal surgery.

It seemed like one horrible situation after another. It wasn't just a one-time surgery; it kept repeating itself, over and over. The pain was nauseating and overwhelming. Most of the time, pain pills wouldn't work for me, and I learned to pray and not focus on my problems because whenever I sensed the presence of the Lord, I often stopped noticing the pain.

But whenever I knew I couldn't handle the pain anymore and was about to go back into the hospital, I would ask the Lord to put me in a room where the other patients needed a touch from Him.

And He did. That prayer helped me come to grips with my condition. It got my mind off of me and onto people who needed the Lord to touch them. I knew an eternal soul was more important than my physical problems, and I wanted to be used by God to save souls.

In difficult situations, I have learned that the most important thing to do is keep your heart right. I had to decide not to become bitter, realizing, "I can be bitter or better, and I choose better." I still say that. During all of the physical problems I was having, I had to believe that somehow, in some way, God was going to bring good out of everything that happened (Romans 8:28).

Today, after eight cervical spine surgeries, six lumbar spine surgeries, and having two twelve-inch steel rods, two plates, and any number of clamps and screws inserted—God remains faithful to me. A few Scriptures in particular give me great comfort:

Nehemiah 8:10: "Neither be ye grieved (sorry), for the joy of the Lord is your strength."

Psalm 16:11: "Thou will show me the path of life, in thy presence is fullness of joy, at thy right hand are pleasures forevermore."

Romans 8:25: "But if we hope for that we see not, then do we with patience wait for it."

God knows and sees all things, and I am fully convinced that what He allows us to go through in this life is nothing compared with the glory that will be revealed in us.

Romans 8:18: "For I reckon that the sufferings of this present time are not worthy to be compared with the glory which shall be revealed in us."

The Peeping Tom

One day when I was praying, I suddenly saw a picture of an American Indian standing in a dry field. The field looked like it had been harvested. All that was left was stubble.

I didn't know why I would see such a thing, but I kept thinking and praying about it. I had a very close friend who lived in the mountains in Chester at the same time Bill and I were there named Billie. She and I knew there was an Assembly of God Native American mission in the area. As we prayed about what I had seen, we felt that we needed to go to Greenville, where one of the missions was located. We had no contacts with the mission and didn't really know what we were doing, so this was a real act of faith for us.

I was driving when we reached Greenville. As we pulled up to the town's only stop sign, I told my friend, "I feel as though we are to turn right." She agreed, so we turned right and continued down the road, which quickly began to take us out of town. When we came to a gas station, I stopped to ask if there is a mission nearby. The attendant told me, "Just keep on this road and you'll come to it on your left."

We eventually arrived at the Greenville Indian Mission, which backed up into a bunch of evergreen trees on the left-hand side of the road. There are always lots of evergreens in the mountains. We climbed out and walked up to the house, and an Indian woman came to the door. Four or five little dark-skinned children peeked around the corner at us.

Some people call it premonitions, but when you have a relationship with God, you realize that He leads you. I really sensed that God wanted to do something at the mission. Even though He hadn't told me so audibly, I felt that He wanted us to have a meeting there. So that's what I told the woman who answered the door. I told her about my vision and that we had driven up from Chico.

She said that her husband, the pastor, was at work at the sawmill, and we should come back later. We were elated at how things were working out and decided that as we waited, we should go get a room at the only hotel in Greenville. It was an old building sitting in a line of other old buildings along the main street.

As we walked inside to check in, my friend and I immediately noticed that something was odd about the desk clerk. Something wasn't right with him, and both we felt like God was warning us that something strange was about to happen.

The clerk handed us a key to a room on the second floor, and Billie and I went upstairs.

The room wasn't large. There was a door on the far wall that I assumed led into a broom closet. As in many buildings in those days, there was a small window over the main door of our room. The window was called a transom, and it went the length of the top of the door with a chain attached to the wall to hold the panel open a few inches and let the air circulate. This was the only ventilation in our room except for the big west-facing window that opened out on the street.

Billie and I removed our blouses because the sun blazing in the window made the room hot and stuffy. We sat on the bed and talked about the day's events and how excited we were to be doing our first evangelistic meeting.

All of a sudden, we heard rattling and movement in the broom closet right next to our room. We hurriedly threw our blouses back on, because we just knew it was the odd little desk clerk. He was the only other person we had seen in the hotel.

My friend, whose mother who had taught her to be afraid of everything, said, "Put the Bible down in front of the door—he won't come in over the Word!"

There are times when God touches you, and you become fearless. Courage rose up in me. I grabbed my Bible and opened the door to the hallway just in time to see the desk clerk dragging a ladder back into the broom closet! I think he had been planning to set it up at our door and peep in at us through the transom.

I felt like my five-foot, two-inch height suddenly shot up to ten feet. I was invincible. Nothing could hurt me. I walked up to the desk clerk, and he fell backward into the closet, the ladder dropping on top of him.

I put my finger on his nose as he lay there on the floor. I was filled with holy anger. "Listen here, mister. God is with us, and you had better leave us alone!"

He started stammering, "B-but ... God ... God ... is ... with meeee, too ..." He was really trying to get the words out and couldn't. He was terrified.

Whirling around, I went back into the room and slammed the door, locking it behind me.

"Oh, my God," Billie was saying. "Oh, my God. Did he get you?"

Obviously, he hadn't. But for at least twenty minutes, the desk clerk walked up and down the hall, muttering, "God's with me, too," over and over again. We could hear him outside the door.

That evening, we returned to the Indian mission. The pastor said, "Yes, that sounds good to have a meeting!"

Billie and I drove back to Chico that night and returned to Chester the following week with our kids. We knew someone who owned a summer home in Chester, and he let us stay there. We ended up having three weeks of meetings, six nights a week. Billie and I took turns preaching and leading worship. The Indians provided the instruments; whoever had a guitar or could play the piano could be a part of the worship team. Many people showed up, and we saw healings and salvations. One Indian woman who couldn't walk without crutches was healed. Caucasians came to the meetings as well.

Penny and Billie's daughter were still small toddlers at that time. The nursery was right off the main building, and we would put them in there, give them each a bottle and say, "Now, go to sleep." And they would. Linda, who was four at the time, would sit on the front row and listen to the preaching.

One woman came to our meetings from the Assembly of God church in nearby Westwood, where she was an associate pastor. One night, we invited her to give a testimony of what God was doing in her life. As she was speaking, she suddenly lifted her hands and declared, "One of these days, God is going to shake Greenville."

At that moment, there was a huge crash. Something big hit the building. The old light bulbs hanging from the ceiling jerked and swung back and forth. The walls shuddered. All the men jumped up and ran outside to see what had happened, and they found a car smashed against the side of the church.

The church sat beside a hill. Apparently, someone had parked his car without setting the brake, and it had rolled down the incline and slammed into the building at exactly the right moment, just as the associate pastor had said, "God is going to shake Greenville."

God certainly had it planned out—her statement and the car's brakes giving way at the right time dramatically proved her point. He likes to do things like that.

Does She Do This All the Time?

I recall another time in Red Bluff when another friend and I attended a revival meeting. It was nearing the end of the meeting, and the speaker was getting tired. He had been preaching really hard, and sweat was rolling down his face. It was one of the last revival meetings he had scheduled for Red Bluff before he went to the next city.

As Lena and I were sitting in the pew, I saw three angels on the platform—two on the right side of the speaker and one on the left. They weren't very clear; I could see them as if through a mist or a veil. I had been taking notes on the sermon, and I quickly wrote a note to Lena telling her what I saw.

The speaker paused his preaching and stepped back from the pulpit. As soon as he did, the angels rushed to him to minister strength. I knew what they were doing by the Holy Spirit, Who had opened my spiritual eyes to know and to be able to see them in the first place. (I might add that I hadn't been asking to see angels or anything like that.) They completely surrounded the minister. I couldn't even see him anymore.

"Oh," he said. "I feel the Lord."

Lena kept the note about the angels until the end of the service. As we went to leave, she showed it to the speaker.

"Does she have this happen all the time?" he asked.

Lena shook her head. "I don't think so," she replied.

He looked at me, and I told him exactly what had happened. I knew they had been ministering strength to him. "When you said, 'I feel the Lord,' that was when the angels were ministering to you" I told him.

That was an entirely new experience for me.

Porterhouse Porcupine

*E*ventually, we moved to the small Northern California town of Whitmore to live on a ranch owned by an attorney who needed a caretaker to look after the property, rent free. The house was new and situated in a meadow with a nice stream flowing along the length of the property. It had never been lived in and wasn't completely finished, but most of the missing elements were fairly minor. It still needed counters in the kitchen, and the windows didn't have any screens.

The first night we stayed in the house, the air was so warm and stuffy that we had to leave a window open. There was a full moon, and in the middle of the night, a loud noise jarred me and Bill awake. Silhouetted in the open window was a raccoon! We'd been awakened by the noise of his claws as he'd scratched and scrambled his way onto the sill. Bill and I hollered, and the noise scared the coon. He jumped back to the ground and ran off. We never had any similar trouble after that, but if memory serves, we had screens put in soon afterward.

The ranch was used to housing varmints and not people. One morning as Bill was leaving for work, he saw a porcupine out by Penny's horse pen. Horses are very curious creatures. If they find an interesting, slow-moving object, they will walk up to check it out. But porcupines can kill horses. If a quill stuck in a horse's nostrils, it will start working up the bony ridge of the horse's head and eventually lodge in the brain. My dad once had to destroy one of our horses because it got a quill in its nose. It is possible to remove them right after it happens, but if one gets up too far, there is nothing to be done to remove it.

Knowing all this, Bill grabbed his .22 rifle and went out and shot the porcupine.

"If I had time, I'd skin it out," he told me. "I've heard that if you're out in the wilderness and had nothing else to eat, this is an easy survival meat to get."

I thought, *Well, I've got time.* I decided to satisfy his curiosity, so I told him I'd skin it. I'd skinned plenty of animals before, helping my dad butcher animals on the ranch. So after Bill left for work, I put on thick leather gloves and carefully carried the porcupine over behind some pussy willows, away from the house.

I got to thinking about the guts and quills and what I was going to do with all of it, so I went back to the house and got a bunch of old newspapers from the back porch and layered them on the ground. I turned the porcupine on its back so I wouldn't have to deal with the quills. Then with pliers in one hand and the skinning knife in the other, I opened up the carcass, cutting from the neck down.

The worst smell in the world slapped me in the face. It was like the worst case of human body odor I'd ever smelled. I wanted to stop and just throw the thing away, but I knew that Bill would always wonder what he had missed by not eating the porcupine meat. So I finished taking out the insides, careful not to cut the gall bladder. Since I grew up on a ranch, helping to slaughter animals, I knew that cutting into the gall bladder makes the meat taste bitter. You have to be careful when you're skinning an animal not to cut into anything internally that could spread fluids into the meat and contaminate it.

When I finished, I took the meat back to the house. There was a cement wash tray on the porch where I washed and soaked the meat in baking soda to get that awful smell out. I soaked it all day, but it kept stinking. *Finally*, several hours later, the evil smell went away, and I put the meat in a pan with onion, garlic, celery, and salt and pepper. Then I covered the whole mess with a piece of foil, stuck it in the oven, and roasted it. I made a completely separate meal for the girls and myself. The porcupine was for Bill, and I was pretty sure we didn't want any.

Bill had to work late that evening, and when he came home, he was brave and ate his porcupine.

"What does it taste like?" I asked.

"Not really much like anything," he replied. Apparently, his wilderness-survival meat had no taste left, and I imagine it was pretty tough after so many hours swimming in baking soda.

"I guess if that's all you had to eat, you could survive," he said.

"Not me," I quipped. "I think I'd go fishing."

The Angels in
the Hospital

*E*ver since the car accident when I nearly went through the windshield, I have dealt with intense, chronic pain. I would regularly check myself into the hospital because the pain didn't respond to most medications, and the only way I had relief was by being hooked up to an IV.

One time when I had checked myself into one of the two major hospitals, two male nurses came and visited me. At least, I *thought* they were male nurses at first. They were dressed in aqua-colored scrubs with white trim around the pockets. One of them hung back by the door, and the other, who was bigger and broader, came up to my bed. He started talking about all of the problems I had been having physically and how they had occurred. He spoke in an odd way. It was as if he had been there for the accident and observed everything that had happened.

"I know how you have suffered and all the excruciating pain you're in," he said. He walked around the bed and put his hand on my forehead. Leaning close to me, he looked into my eyes and said, "But everything is going to be all right." He said it with such finality that I knew everything *was* going to be all right.

Something was different about his eyes. It's hard to describe. Spiritual things are never easy to describe with natural words. I had never seen eyes like his before; they were such a dark brown, and I realized as I was looking at him that they weren't normal eyes. They weren't earthly at all.

He walked out of the room with the other man, who stayed at the door during the whole encounter, and they closed the door behind them. I lay there for a while thinking about what had just happened. Eventually, I called for my doctor, who was a Christian, and told him about the "men" who had paid me a visit. By then, I felt so much better that we talked about me getting discharged.

The God of Money

*I*n the late 1960s, we were living in Redding, and I started attending a weekly ladies' Bible study and prayer meeting. After one of these meetings, a friend of mine said, "I'm going to go home and put on Family Radio."

"What is that?" I asked.

"That's a Christian radio station," she replied.

She gave me the number on the AM band dial for the station KVIP. I started listening to it, and I really liked it. Little did I know at the time that God was moving in my heart for something He wanted to do as an outreach for the outlying communities.

A few years later, Bill and I went up to Surprise Valley to attend my uncle's funeral in Eagleville. We arrived early, before the rest of the family got there, and I felt pressed upon by the Holy Spirit to pray, so Bill and I drove over to Alkali Lake. It was a "country mile" or two away from the funeral.

We parked on the southern end of the valley and stood outside the car, looking north. This was the valley where I had been born, and I dearly loved it. We began to pray for the souls of the ranchers and the people living in it such as my family, who had not heard the truth of the Gospel when I was a child.

Suddenly, I felt like God spoke to me about getting a radio translator into the valley. A translator is a receiver that catches the broadcast signal so people in the area can listen to the station. Not many people had experienced Jesus in the valley, and I knew it was a "dark" place. But changes were coming.

As if He didn't already know, I said to the Lord, "I don't have the money (to build a radio translator), but I'll do it with Your help."

When we returned to Redding, I called KVIP and talked to the station manager, asking him what it would cost to get a translator put into Surprise Valley. He told me, and I was stunned. It was a huge amount.

"I don't have the money," I told him, "but I know God said to go for it."

As I began to pray about the finances and what I could do, the Lord told me to talk about the translator for Surprise Valley with the people He showed me. So I told Christian doctors, dentists, and other people what I wanted to do, and in a relatively short amount of time, God brought in the money for the Cedarville translator. All of it was sent in to KVIP, and they were able to cover the full cost.

Then came the long wait to get the okay from the Federal Communications Commission (FCC), as well as find a physical location for the translator.

Months passed. I began to get a little impatient because it was taking so long. When the Lord lays something on your heart, you want to get up and get it done. He had provided the money— and it would be done, but I sure didn't like the wait. The Lord has His own schedule and I needed to be still, pray, and wait on His per- fect timing.

One day I got a call from a woman who worked at KVIP. "The station manager told me to call you and let you know that the Cedarville translator is going on the air," she said.

Praise God! A victory at last. The radio signal could be heard all over the valley, even on the tops of the mountains. This allowed ranchers like my family, who gathered around and listened to the radio together, to hear about God twenty-four hours a day. The sta- tion carried Christian music and the preaching of the Word back into the canyons. It was an awesome victory for the Lord and continues its ministry to this day, bringing His love, grace, and salvation to the far-flung communities in Northern California.

Our Wild Move to Washington

*a*round 1968, we became acquainted with a family at church who was having prayer meetings at their home. After a few months, this family moved north up to Washington. We didn't hear from them for a couple of months, but I began to feel a tug in my heart and wondered if God was getting ready to move us to Washington, too.

Bill was working at the Kimberly Clark Pulp and Paper Mill. He was a heavy equipment mechanic, and it was a good job with good pay and benefits. I told him what I was sensing, and we began to pray about moving to Washington.

"If You're leading us there," I asked the Lord, "would You have our friends, Frank and Zena, send us a letter of invitation?"

Just a few days later, a letter from our friends was sitting in the mailbox. Zena had written, "Why don't you come up to Washington to see what God is doing up here?"

It was springtime, near Easter vacation, and Bill and I both felt that Penny and I should go "spy out the land," so to speak. We prayed the whole way, asking the Lord, "Is it yes or is it no, that we should move up here to Washington?"

Repeatedly, we asked for confirmation. The Bible says that out of the mouth of two or three witnesses a thing shall be established—and we needed this to be established! For that big of a move, we really wanted it to be the Lord's will, not our own. Bill would be leaving a good job, and Penny would have to change schools. And we were native Californians who had never lived anywhere else.

We arrived at our friends' house in Selleck on Saturday night, and the next day, we drove the forty miles down to Tacoma to go to Sunday school and church. A lady who was teaching the adult Sunday school class came and introduced herself to Penny and me when she was finished.

"The strangest thing happened as I was teaching this morning," she said. "I have never had anything like this happen before, but as I was teaching, the Lord gave me a vision. There was a businessman dressed in a suit, sitting at a desk and writing out a decision, and it was 'Yes.'"

She asked if that meant anything to us.

"Yes!" we answered, and we told her about how we had come to Washington from California asking God over and over again, "Is it yes or is it no?"

That was our first confirmation about the move. Before leaving Washington to go back to California, we received two more. It could not have been made more obvious. When we returned to Redding, Penny and I told Bill about how the Lord had confirmed the move. We notified our friends in Selleck that we were coming so they could help us. Then Bill took his vacation, and he and I returned to Selleck, to look for work.

The day after we arrived, Bill went down to Tacoma, where Frank introduced him to the church pastor, Pastor Yersted.

A short time after they left, Mrs. Yersted said to her husband, "Why don't you find a job for Brother Bill?"

He said, "Well ... okay," and got out the phone book and turned to the yellow pages. He looked under the section for raw material handlers. As he was thumbing through the pages, an ad jumped out at him. It was for a local air service company. He called, and a man answered.

"Hello, I am Pastor Yersted from Faith Tabernacle. Do you need a mechanic?" he asked.

The man said, "Yes, we do. Are you a mechanic also?"

"No, I am not, but I know a man who is."

"Well, have him come in, and fill out an application right away."

The pastor called just as Bill and Frank were walking in the door. As a result of the conversation, they had to turn around and drive the forty miles back to Tacoma, where Bill filled out the application for the company and had a physical as well. He was hired immediately and went to work the next day.

God is always looking out for us, and I firmly believe if He calls us to do something, He will confirm it more than one way; we only need to ask and then wait on Him for confirmation. If we are faithful and stay in His Word and pray, He will always answer, for He is above all others. Our Father in Heaven knows what is best for His children.

The House with the Barn and the Pasture

*F*aith Tabernacle in Tacoma held services in an old movie theater downtown. They had remodeled the projection room into a small apartment where itinerant ministers could stay.

The apartment wasn't being used at the time, so Pastor Yersted let Bill stay there since it wasn't far from his new job. Meanwhile, Penny and I returned to Redding to start packing. We had been praying about the specific type of house we wanted in Washington. It needed to include a barn and a pasture because Penny had her horse, a three-year-old Arabian mare she had trained herself (with a little help from me).

When Bill came down to Redding to help us move, I asked with much confidence, "You found a house to rent with a barn, didn't you?"

But he hadn't. "There were hardly any rentals in all the large Tacoma papers," he replied.

I was surprised that there wasn't anything to rent in a city that big, but I had no doubt, not one little bit, that God had the exact house, barn, and pasture Penny and I had been praying for.

We rented a big commercial rental truck, filled it with our stuff, and used it to pull our ski boat. Bill drove the truck while I drove our car, pulling the horse trailer. We were off on our Washington adventure.

Bill had found a temporary place to leave the horse, trailer, and boat just south of Tacoma. We dropped them off and got into town late Saturday night, parking on a side street up from the church.

We were all tired from the fourteen-hour trip, which had been especially long and draining for us because we'd had to break at every rest stop to let the horse out and give her some exercise. We fell into our beds in the church's small apartment and slept well—until the doors opened the next morning, and we heard the people starting to come in for church.

Immediately, Bill got dressed and went out to purchase a newspaper to see about a house. We looked through the paper, and guess what? There were only two houses to rent.

We couldn't even find the first house. We got lost, and then when we finally found the place, it wasn't anything like what we'd prayed for. There wasn't a barn, and the house wasn't in the best shape. Not wanting to get lost again, we stopped and called the owners of the next house, asking for directions. The rental was outside the town of Puyallup.

We drove out on Canyon Road, and as we made the last turn, there it was—a house, a barn, and a fenced pasture. Exactly what we had been praying for! We chatted with the owners and mentioned the trouble we'd been having finding a place. Bill had been working in Tacoma for a week, and there hadn't been any house rentals listed in the paper.

The couple, Gayle and Dorothy, had just purchased the rental house. They'd moved it onto their property, which was right across the road from their own lovely home. This was the first day their ad had been in the paper.

"Our daughter has a horse," Bill told Gayle. "Are the barn and pasture yours?"

Gayle nodded. "Yes, but I'm not sure if the fences are stable. Why don't you come check them out with me?"

Dorothy later told me that she was surprised her husband had rented to someone who had a horse. He didn't even like horses, she said.

When God is directing you, He will answer prayers prayed in faith. We had been praying for something specific, and He answered specifically. We lived in Washington for two years, and God ended up being in the move much more than anything we had expected. It was good we got out of Redding when we did because the employees at Bill's old job went on strike soon after he left. The strike lasted for so long that many of the employees lost their homes. God moved us up to Washington right on time.

Bill didn't get vacation time with his new company, but the job itself was better. He had his own truck and would drive from Tacoma to service equipment in towns along the coast. The trips lasted several days, and I often would travel with him and keep him company.

God is so good. He brings great adventures into a person's life. Psalm 75:6 says, "For promotion cometh not from the east, nor from the west, nor from the south." The only place left out of that verse is *north*, and to the north was where God led us.

The Unexpected Hawaiian Adventure

*W*e had been living in Puyallup for about two years when suddenly, something happened.

Penny was about to graduate from Puyallup High School, and she was praying about what to do after that—but none of us knew that. One day she ran into the house after school.

"Mom! Mom!" she said. "I know what I am supposed to do with my life after I graduate."

"Oh? What is it?" I asked.

Penny was really excited—God had told her to go to Hawaii and get a job.

I almost laughed like Sarah did in the Bible when God told her she was going to have a baby at ninety. I thought it was comical. So off the wall.

Managing to keep my laughter to myself, I said, "Okay. Well, we will pray about it."

As we prayed about the Lord's leading for Penny, He spoke to us that we were *all* move to Hawaii. Needless to say, we were all very surprised.

A few **years** earlier, we had met a pastoring couple who lived in Honolulu. When we really knew that God was in this big move across the ocean, we decided to contact them to see if they could help Bill get a job.

Pastor Jack was a mechanic, too, and said he was sure that Bill could find employment with the company he worked for—an inter-island equipment company which repaired name-brand lawn-mowers and other things. Bill had a job as soon as we moved.

Bill made two large shipping crates so we could send over our personal belongings and his tools. We sold all our furniture to the landlord and, sadly, Penny sold her horse. Linda shipped her car along with the crates we sent.

So it was off to Hawaii for the whole family after Penny graduated from high school. We found a duplex just outside Pearl City on the island of Oahu. Bill had to ride the bus into Honolulu every day to work because it took three weeks for the ship to arrive with the car.

We didn't live in the lap of luxury when we first arrived. There were struggles of everyday life, but we were still all together, depending on the Lord for strength. While waiting for Bill's first paycheck, we slept on air mattresses that leaked. Each morning, we would wake up on the hard concrete floor. We bought mattresses as soon as we could. We had made the mistake of not shipping our refrigerator, so as we were waiting for the car to arrive, we had to walk down to Pearl City nearly every day, purchase bags of ice for our styrofoam ice chests, and then carry them home. The ice would start to melt on the way back, so we would fill the chests with cubes, water, and slush. It was pretty sad.

"Lord, we need a refrigerator," we prayed.

We heard about a flea market that the military hosted a few blocks out of Pearl City every Saturday. It opened at 7 a.m., and by the time we got there, there was a large crowd of people waiting outside the gate, many of them looking for a refrigerator, too. Everyone had numbered tags so you could claim whatever you wanted to buy. As soon as the gates opened, we started running. We managed to tag a refrigerator, and after that, our lives dramatically improved— no more carrying ice from the store on foot.

After getting suntans and learning a little pidgin English, we slowly began to fit into the Hawaiian culture a little better.

We attended Pastor Jack's church in Honolulu. It was a small church, probably around sixty people. As word got around that we didn't have our car yet, a brother from the church loaned us an extra car he had. Penny bought herself a car with the money she received from selling her horse and got a job on Waikiki selling tourist trinkets from a cart every night. Linda was a dental assistant by trade, and she started working for a dentist in Honolulu.

Before long, we had a house full of girls who wanted to live with us. Most of them were Penny and Linda's friends, who had followed us from the mainland. They slept on the horrible air mattresses on the floor, and we would talk to them about Jesus.

One day, Linda and Penny went to the beach to go swimming. When they came home, they announced, "Mom, we found us a brother." The girls had always wanted a brother.

It was a Navy boy from Washington State who was stationed at Pearl Harbor. His name was Jim. The girls met him on the beach and decided to invite him over to meet Bill. He and Bill had a good connection because they both owned motorcycles—so they had something in common to talk about.

Jim was a Godsend for us. This was the beginning of a life-long friendship. Some friends are friends for a brief time, and then they go, but Jim never left. He still calls me several times a month.

Jim and Bill would often go on long motorcycle rides together. One day, they turned off the main road and came upon a deserted pineapple field. They stopped and discovered that the picking machine hadn't been able to harvest the pineapples in the corners of the field, so those were still full of fruit. They picked as many leftover pineapples as they could carry in their shirts and then came home with their treasures. We had a wonderful feast of the most delicious pineapples we had ever eaten. Even now, my mouth waters just thinking about it!

We loved living in Pearl City. The inter-island company my husband worked for would send him to other islands every month to service the equipment. He was given an expense account, a rental car, a hotel room, and meals. I would buy my own plane ticket and go with him. When he was at work, I would take the rental car and explore whatever island we were on. Once on Maui, I traveled up a steep, winding road to the dormant Haleakala Crater. When Bill got off work, we drove back and watched the sunset from the top of the crater. It was beautiful.

We lived in Pearl City for two years. It was a time of ministry—and beach trips!

The Time We Were Almost Mugged

*P*enny and I often went to Nanakuli Beach to go swimming, where a three-winged school building sat a stone's throw away. School was out for the summer, but the beach was fairly remote, so it was usually empty. On that particular day, I don't remember anyone being on the beach with us.

We put out our towels, and Penny walked down to the water and started swimming. I was sunbathing and enjoying the scenery when I suddenly noticed two boys near our car. It was fairly common in those days to have your car broken into. If you locked the car, the thieves broke windows, so we actually left Penny's car unlocked because there wasn't anything in it of value.

I tried to get Penny's attention, but she didn't see me, and the ocean covered up the sound of my voice. So by myself, I gathered our purses and towels and started walking back toward the car.

As I approached the parking lot, I could see the boys looking into the car.. *I have to move the car,* I thought, so I could keep a better eye on it.

As I walked toward the car with my arms full, I began to feel righteously indignant. How dare those boys try to break into our car! I was going to give them a piece of my mind. But then, all of a sudden, I found myself walking in the opposite direction—back toward the beach. I moved without thought, my body listening to a still, small voice my ears did not hear. I had no idea what I was doing. I just knew I needed to go back, something prompting my spirit that I needed to change my direction.

I walked past a wing of the school, and as I got to the end of the classroom wall, one of the boys walked around the corner. He jerked back violently, obviously startled to see me. I knew what he had intended—to mug me and take the purses I was carrying. And likely would have, if I hadn't doubled back.

It all happened so quickly. I ran back to the car, moving it around the school and closer to the beach, where we were. Penny came out of the water to find out what was happening. I brought her up to speed about the boys and then calmly spread the towels out again as she returned to swimming.

A few minutes passed. Then once again, as I was sitting on the beach, I looked at the car, and I saw that one of the boys had returned. I sprinted through the sand and thorn trees so fast that I seemed to have winged feet. I was righteously indignant and I yelled at the boy, "GET AWAY FROM MY CAR!"

He took off, and I chased him clear across Kamehameha Highway into a residential area. Eventually, he got away from me, and when I heard dogs barking viciously, I knew he was somebody else's problem. So I went back to the beach. This was another one of those times when I felt like I was invincible because Jesus was with me!

The Time I Talked
to the Thief

*W*hile we were living in Pearl City, Bill's dad had a heart attack and had to have surgery. Bill took a leave of absence, and he and I flew over to the mainland to spend time with his father, who lived in Clear Lake Highlands, California. A dear friend of ours lived not too far away in Sacramento, and we decided to go visit her before we returned to Hawaii.

While we were at her house, I happened to look through her copy of the newspaper and found a notice for a nurse's aide training course subsidized by the government. Students had to pay for their textbooks but otherwise, the government covered all expenses.

I felt that being a nurse's aide was something I wanted to do, so I asked Bill what he thought of returning to Hawaii on his own while I stayed in Sacramento and trained as a nurse's aide? The girls were no longer small and I had always wanted to be a nurse. In fact, I used to play at being a nurse when I was a child. He agreed that it would be fine if I stayed for school and he went back to the islands to work, and that's how I became a student again.

The course started off with several weeks of in-school study that focused on the medical terminology and nursing procedures, and then we worked in two different convalescent hospitals. In pairs, we would be assigned two patients, whom we would look after for a couple of days, and then we would be assigned two new patients.

One afternoon, I heard some visitors talking to one of the patients. He wasn't one of mine, but I knew about him. He had been shot in a robbery gone bad—and he was the thief. The bullet had severed his spinal cord, making him a quadriplegic—paralyzed from the neck down.

The visitors were talking to him about coming to know Jesus, but he wasn't receiving it very well. I felt as if the visitors were going about it all wrong, and I thought, *If I ever get him as a patient, I'm going to try a different approach than what they are trying.*

Eventually, my turn came to care for that man. My instructor told us they didn't expect him to live very long because he kept getting infections from his ileostomy (a procedure where the abdominal wall is opened up and part of the intestine drains digestive matter into a bag placed on the outside of the body).

The instructor also warned us to watch out, because the only thing that patient could do was chew tobacco. So they let him have that little vice, but he had a serious anger problem and would spit tobacco juice on his nurse's uniform if he became frustrated.

"He did it to me," my instructor said, "so anybody who gets him as a patient—watch out!"

I went into the patient's room and introduced myself. "I'm Mrs. Arnold," I said. "I'm from Hawaii, and I'm here to be your nurse for a few days."

The man didn't talk to me at all. He didn't even say hello, so I just talked as I bathed him and changed his bedding. I talked a lot during those two days, but oddly, I didn't feel like I was supposed to give him any kind of testimony about Jesus while caring for him. So I just carried on a long, one-sided conversation during my time with him.

After we students had been at that convalescent hospital for a while, we were transferred to another rehabilitation hospital in north Sacramento, and I wouldn't see that patient anymore. Before we left, I prayed, "Lord, now I feel like I'm supposed to talk to him about Jesus." Technically, I was not supposed to share my faith while I was at work; we weren't supposed to talk about our religious views with our patients. I knew that. "How do I go about talking to this man?" I asked.

As I prayed about the issues involved, the Lord told me to go in as a visitor and gave me a specific day. That day came, and the Lord spoke to my heart and said, "Tonight is the night." So I drove over to the hospital and went up to the man's room.

When I arrived, I saw that all the lights were off, and I thought, *Oh, goodness. He's asleep.* But I decided to go in anyway. I called him by name and said, "This is Mrs. Arnold. The Lord sent me in here to talk to you." There's nothing like just being honest.

"Well, He must have," the man replied. I was so surprised because it was the first time he had ever spoken to me. I learned later that he thought I had gone back to Hawaii because he hadn't seen me in a week.

We talked about my being back at the hospital, and then I told him how I had been a Christian for a good many years and how Jesus loved me and had brought me to know Him. I shared my testimony with him, the story of how I had given my heart to the Lord. "The Lord wants me to tell you that He loves you in spite of anything that has happened to you in your past," I said. "He really wants you to know that He loves you. That is just really important for you to know. When Jesus was on the cross, He forgave a thief who was dying right next to Him. When the thief asked Jesus to remember him when He came into His kingdom, Jesus told him, 'Today you will be with Me in paradise.' That thief right next to Him was forgiven. Jesus can do the same thing with you. He loves you so much."

I asked the man if he wanted to give his heart to Jesus, and he said yes. So we prayed the Sinner's Prayer.

At the end of our time together, I said, "Well, I need to go now. If I don't see you again down here, on this earth, I expect to see you in Heaven because you gave your heart to the Lord just now."

"Well," he replied, "you know there's two places, don't you?"

"I know that! But you're not going to Hell. You're going to Heaven now, because you gave your heart to Jesus. You have a good life, and the Lord bless you. Good night."

I left that night knowing that God always has perfect timing and if I listen to His voice, His purposes will be revealed. I may never know what happened to that patient on this side of Heaven, but I know we will meet again in the presence of the Lord.

Hawaii 2.0

*O*ur time in Hawaii was wonderful. Young people from the mainland would come and stay with us, and it was a blessing to be able to pour into their lives.

After living in Pearl City for two years, we began to sense a draw in our hearts to go somewhere else. We ended up heading back to the mainland and the Redding area due to my continuing health issues. Before long, however, it became evident that we wouldn't be staying in Redding long term. Bill's job didn't pay what he had been making in Hawaii, and there just wasn't much work to be found. And we still had that feeling that we needed to go south of Oahu.

So I suggested to Bill that he call his former boss in Pearl City and ask if he could be hired back.

His boss was excited because Bill had a lot of expertise in many areas. "Come on back, and we will put you in Hilo on the Big Island," he said, which "just so happened" to be south of Oahu.

So we moved back to the islands. We rented a studio apartment right on the waterfront of Hilo Lagoon, just across the street from Bill's work. In the "winter" months, it had a very nice view. You could look up from the tropics to the snow-capped mountains of Mauna Loa and Mauna Kea. We were also really close to the docks, so when the cruise ships came in, the people standing on the deck would wave at us.

Our apartment was only a short distance from the hotels along the Hilo Lagoon. They had beautiful grounds, with picnic tables and benches, coconut palms and other beautiful flowering trees. We often would go down there to barbecue steaks and clams and dip them in garlic butter. As tourists passed us, they would comment on how delicious the barbecue smelled.

"Thank you," we'd say. "We do this pretty often."

"Do you live here?" we'd be asked.

"Oh, yes."

"How great that must be," was by and large the reply.

And, of course, we would agree that it was really wonderful.

One day, Bill came back from the waterfront and said, "Come out. I have something to show you."

We went out to the water's edge, and Bill showed me a large sea turtle someone had caught. They'd put a hole in the edge of its shell and tied it with fishing line to some bushes along in the water. The turtle was struggling to get free. Bill, who always carried a pocketknife, cut the fish line and let the turtle go. We assumed that whoever had caught it was planning on having turtle for dinner. Well, their meal was quite happy as it swam back out into the ocean.

Behind our apartment complex, there was a large jungle area that was owned by some Japanese people. You couldn't see any of the buildings due to the jungle cover, but every Saturday night, they threw a huge party. We could hear their loud laughing and talking, and at the end of the night as the partygoers left, they would all shout, *"Banzai! Banzai! Banzai!"* We assumed it was a Japanese toast.

We attended a church in a small sugar-cane town called Pepeekeo, and the pastor sometimes asked me to preach on Sunday nights. We enjoyed going to that little church, and in a short time, we made some really good friends. The Hawaiian people are wonderful. Bill serviced the equipment at a sugar cane mill north of Pepeekeo, and he would have to drive out through the tall cane fields to get to it.

We left Hawaii the first time because of my health issues, and the pain in my back slowly grew worse until, for about a month and a half, I was bedridden. There was nothing I could do but lie there, and I found myself beginning to feel more and more afraid. Normally, I am not a fearful person, but this fear took hold of me and I couldn't get it to stop. There wasn't a reason for it, and I didn't understand why I felt that way.

I finally began to snap out of it, and I asked God what it was. He replied, "I am letting you feel what the people on these islands feel." The Hawaiian people suffer from extreme superstitions, and I knew that darkness was trying to torment them and keep them in bondage. This experience gave me greater insight into how to minister to the people around me. Many of them still believe in Pele, the Hawaiian fire goddess, because of the volcanoes. It was not uncommon to see what I assumed to be flower offerings set on fence posts to appease the goddess. There were also small Buddhist temples built like small lath shacks. You could look between the laths and see small Buddhist idols with offerings of fruit and other food products. This was during the 1970s when hippies were living on the beaches, and they would break into the small idol-worshipping temples and steal the food. It seemed the hippies thought it was fine to eat the offerings to the temple since Buddha never ate them.

After God spoke to me to explain why He allowed my fearfulness, the fear passed completely. I wasn't afraid anymore and I understood the culture better.

Fire on the Mountain!

One day while I was at the doctor's office, the island of Hilo shook with an earthquake. I heard plate glass windows breaking in the storefronts up and down the street. They shattered and fell in chunks onto the sidewalk. The doctor had a shelf lined with antique medicine bottles, and as the earth shuddered, the bottles jumped up and down. I was sitting right under the shelf. As the bottles started falling past my head and smashing near my feet, I jumped up and tried to run out of the office to a safer place.

The doctor himself was in a panic. He kept running back and forth and saying in broken English, "I need to call my wife! I need to call my wife!" He was a Japanese doctor, and he spoke English very well but, in the excitement, his accent became worse. I could barely understand him. I found out later that he had gone through an earthquake before, as well as a subsequent tsunami. That was what he was concerned about—his home was right there on the waterfront, and he was afraid for his wife and his house.

He was frantic, but he kept his wits about him enough to stop me from leaving by myself. "You're under the influence!" he said. He'd given me medication for the pain in my body, and I wasn't safe to drive.

Wanting to get home myself, I replied, "I'll go by cab."

The earth was still shaking. Patients were running out into the street. It seemed like the quake went on for a long time, but in

150

reality, I think it lasted for less than a minute. I managed to find a taxi and got back to our apartment.

Bill got home shortly after I did. Everything had been shut down at his job. When the earthquake started, he and his coworkers were working beneath large caterpillar tractors set up on blocks. The tractors started jumping around and the crew scattered, running out of the building.

The building had a concrete floor, and Bill told me that the earthquake felt like a sledgehammer hitting the bottoms of their feet.

The community of Hilo is familiar with earthquakes. A rock wall runs around the lagoon to help protect the town from tsunamis, which had destroyed schools and other buildings in the past. Downtown Hilo is right beside the lagoon, only about fifteen feet away from the water. After a large earthquake in 1960, the water in the lagoon had retreated, leaving scores of fish jumping around on the sand. Some crazy people had gone out to collect them, and when the tsunami came crashing in, they lost their lives. Fortunately, there was no tsunami with this quake.

We found out that the earthquake was caused by the eruption of the Kilauea volcano. The volcano remained active for about three months, which made our lives very interesting! But during one of its quieter times, we went to investigate. We drove up the mountain and looked around at the damage. Volcanologists kept a close eye on the mountain and had much of it taped off, trying to keep people from doing dumb things that were dangerous. They weren't always successful. People liked to cross the barriers and stick silver dollars in the still-hot lava. Then as the lava cooled, they would cut the silver dollars out and take the chunks of lava home as trophies.

One of our favorite places to go on the island was a natural phenomenon called the Queen's Bath—an area full of coconut palms and warm puddles of water. It was a nice place to walk around in. After we moved away from Hilo, Kilauea erupted again and destroyed the Queen's Bath, as well as several homes that had been built in the area. Kilauea has been erupting continuously since 1983.

Pat standing by the hardened lava from the 1973 Kilauea Volcano eruption.

The Second Return from Hawaii

*a*s time went on, my physical problems became more acute. I never fully recovered from that car accident in the '60s. We decided that because of the deterioration of my spine, it would be best to move back to Redding for better medical attention. So after two years of living in Hilo, we returned to California.

For a short time, we lived with our daughter Linda and son-in-law Sam, and kept an eye on the paper for a house to buy. Eventually, we found a mobile home for sale in Jones Valley, a beautiful area near Lake Shasta. When we talked to the owners, we discovered they were selling it fully furnished, which we desperately needed. It had been their summer home, so they were getting rid of everything, when we didn't have anything. We had left most of our household items in Washington. This house was definitely a blessing from the Lord.

Bill looked for work in Redding, and our former pastor, who was a Greyhound driver, told him, "Why don't you put your application in for a mechanic's job at Greyhound?" So Bill applied, and he was immediately hired to work the night shift. He serviced and made small repairs to the buses as they came in.

But it wasn't easy for him to work the graveyard shift, and the hours began to take a toll on him. By the time Friday rolled around each week, he would feel ill, as if he had the flu. He had a hard time coming home from work and then going to bed when the sun was up.

"You need to go to bed," I would tell him.

"I need to do just one more thing," he would answer. He wasn't getting enough sleep.

I told an elderly friend in our Wednesday prayer group that Bill was feeling sick every weekend. She was a sweet woman of God in her eighties, and she replied, "Well, we will just pray that he gets a day job."

"There is no day job except the boss's job," I said, but we prayed anyway that God would create a job for Bill.

A short time later, Bill's boss asked if he could come in during the day to help him, and Bill accepted right away.

It is amazing what God will do when you ask for His help. I have seen Him move in our lives again and again, and He always amazes me.

Two months after Bill began to work regular day hours, I started feeling that something was not right at the bus depot with his boss. I recognized this feeling as something given to me from the Lord, and I asked Him what was going on. As I prayed about it, I felt strongly led to ask God to reveal what was going on in Phoenix Towers, which was the headquarters for Greyhound at the time, as well as the regional boss in San Francisco.

Three weeks later, our phone rang and when I answered, Bill's boss asked, "Is Bill home? Have him come in right away." He sounded like there had been a death in the family.

When Bill arrived at the depot, the boss from San Francisco was there. "I want you to take over being in charge of the shop," the man said, "because your boss has been fired."

The Lord takes care of His children, and He is always faithful. He not only gave Bill the day job but also promoted him until he finally retired.

God, the Surgeon

*A*fter we moved back to the mainland, I began to get really sick. I dropped down to eighty-four pounds. The doctor did a special scan, and the results showed that I had a pancreatic tumor. In those days, such a tumor was usually fatal. There wasn't any treatment, so the doctors just sent me home. Nothing could be done.

My "prayer closet" back then happened to be the bathroom. As soon as Bill and I got back to the house, I immediately went into the bathroom and closed the door. I prayed, "Lord, give me a Scripture that I can stand on."

When I opened up my Bible, my eyes fell on Psalm 118:17, which says, "I shall not die but live and declare the mighty works of God." By the Holy Spirit, I felt assurance came into my heart, and soon afterward, all my symptoms left. I started gaining weight, and to this day I've had no reoccurrence of the problem.

Soon after God removed the tumor from my pancreas, I found a large lump in my breast. I went to the doctor on a Friday, and he examined it and said, "We will have to do a mammogram."

Unfortunately, no appointment was available until the following Monday. So I went home and prayed and read my Bible, putting my faith in God and His Word and His promises.

On Monday when I went in for the mammogram, the technician told me to show her the lump. I searched my breast, since I knew where it was from my visit to the doctor just a few days before, but I couldn't find it.

"It doesn't seem to be there anymore," I said to the lab technician.

She handed me a marker.

"Here. Mark where it used to be," she said.

I did, and the mammogram results were negative. I realized I had been healed again.

The Gold Miner and Specific Prayer

One of our favorite places to go in the Redding area was Whiskeytown Lake. Eventually, we moved to a mobile park in French Gulch, a small town nearly right on the lake. It was established during the famous California Gold Rush days, with a post office, hotel, and Catholic church. I think the old stagecoach line used to drive through the area.

A stream called Clear Creek ran along the edge of the mobile park. It flowed past the little settlement of French Gulch, and back in the day, people would search along the stream for gold. During the warm months, I would roll up my pant legs and go out to pan for gold with my wok. The wok worked pretty well because it had a handle on each side. I also had a hook that I would use to dig between the rocks and pull out small gold nuggets sometimes. I had a lot of fun during the summer, and I actually found enough gold to fill a film canister. We lived in French Gulch for one or two summers while Bill was the boss at Greyhound. Those were my Gold Rush days!

When fishing season started, I got my fishing license and went into town to buy bait and a pole. Bill didn't care much for fishing, but I loved it. When I was a child, my father's property had a stream, and I was always fishing with a long piece of string and willow sticks.

One day while I was out with my pole, I prayed, "Lord, I want a fish!" I kept praying those words, hoping for a trout, and pretty soon, I felt a tug on the line and pulled out a suckerfish. It's similar to a catfish, but I think the locals call it a cowfish. I caught four or five cowfish, all the while praying, "Lord, I want a fish!"

Finally, He replied quite clearly, "Be specific!"

So I said, "Lord, I want a trout!"

The next fish I pulled out of the stream was a trout. This taught me to be detailed when I'm praying and to tell God exactly what I want. He likes to give His kids what they ask for. Even though He is God and already knows our desires before we ask, being detailed in prayer is important. It's a lifelong lesson and habit His kids ought to keep, proving God hears our every prayer.

The Picketer

This story occurred on old Bechelli Lane, when Bethel Church was located in downtown Redding near the Sacramento River. We had just started attending Bethel, and the church had acquired a protesting picketer. He walked up and down the sidewalk in front of the building and carried a huge sign emblazoned with very hateful things about the church. He drew the eyes of everyone who passed by, and the signs were pretty shocking. One day, the pastor's wife felt sorry for him because it was so hot, so she took him a soft drink. He threw the drink on her inside her car and scared her pretty badly.

The church did everything it could to make the man stop. He had been counseled and spoken to, but it hadn't helped. If there is anything I've learned during ministry, it is that you never counsel people who are listening to dark spirits. Jesus never saw someone who was demon-possessed and said, "Let's talk about it, and I'll counsel you." No, He always cast the spirit out. This person was obviously filled with a spirit of hatred and bitterness, and those are not of God.

I was infuriated about his sign. I knew this was an attack on the church, and it annoyed me that people didn't seem to take it all that seriously. "Has anyone prayed against this man?" I asked another woman at the church.

"Yes," she replied. "We prayed. The church has done everything they can."

"Then why is he still here?" I asked.

I prayed about the situation, and the Lord showed me that I should do a prayer walk in front of the church, right where the man usually picketed. The man thought that was his territory, but I was filled with certainty he wasn't going to take it back. For several months, Bill drove me to the church early every Saturday morning, and I walked back and forth by myself, praying. One of Bethel's pastors found out about my solo prayer walk and made an announcement from the pulpit, asking if anyone wanted to join me. No one did.

Finally, about the time Bethel was going to move to the new College View location, the church placed a restraining order on the picketer. He couldn't even go on the driveway to the property anymore, so he tried to do his picketing up and down Churn Creek Road instead. People could see him picketing because there was a great deal of traffic. His messages were still on the signs, but something was lost in translation and it must have frustrated him, because he didn't keep it up for long after that. God can be dramatic but sometimes He is more subtle. I believe it was the constant prayer and act of reclaiming the ground as God's, in addition to the other legal action, that defeated this enemy of the church. It was a combination punch.

When God tells you to do something, you should always stick with what He tells you to do. I prayed as He showed me to pray, and the church did what it could do in the natural (got a restraining order) and the picketing finally stopped.

The Time I Prayed at the Topless Bar

*L*ater, Bill and I moved from French Gulch into Redding, where we lived near Hilltop Drive. One day as Bill and I drove past a bar and restaurant on Hilltop, I felt the Lord tell me to pray against it. It was one of the worst areas for drug dealing in town, and our mobile park was just a hop and a skip away. Every night when the bar closed, the patrons would get into their cars and drive down the long dusty road to the street. Redding is high desert, and the vacant lot where the bar patrons parked was essentially a dustbowl. The dust would billow like a storm in the Sahara, roll across the road, and settle on all the mobiles, cars, trees, and plants in our park.

Every time we drove by the bar, I prayed against it. I had no idea how God was going to close the place, but I knew He had a plan. I asked that He would put a nice building there instead of a bar.

There was a large sign set up on the hill so it could be seen from a nearby road the locals called Miracle Mile, which is a main thoroughfare. It was an advertisement to draw patrons to the bars on Hilltop Drive. The sign was in sections, and each section had a letter that spelled out the name of the bar. One by one, those letters began to drop off.

Just a few weeks after the Lord told me to pray about the bar, the letters were gone. In due time, and with much prayer, finally the place closed up and the building was condemned and was torn down.

A bonus from the Lord was this: After the bar was torn down, a developer built some nice office buildings at that very location. I don't believe the new offices were accidental. God is faithful when we listen to His promptings and are obedient to His Word.

Another time, the Lord spoke to me about a topless dance bar on Lake Boulevard that the nearby residents didn't like. God led me to start praying about the bar's closure. He gave me the same instructions He had given me about the picketer and the other bar's closure—I needed to go to the site and pray.

When I first told Bill about the plan, he was a little alarmed. He seemed to think it was more *my* plan, not God's.

"Don't you think," he asked, "the police might come by and see you walking around and wonder what you're doing there?"

"Well, we'll go early in the morning on Saturday, and there won't be much traffic. People won't look at me. They'll just think I'm looking at the building."

So every Saturday morning, I would walk around the topless bar in the parking lot and pray. I asked God to do whatever He wanted to do—that He would close it up. I exercised my authority in Christ's name over the darkness.

Several weeks later, a story came out in the town paper. The headline declared, "The Days of the Topless Bar on Lake Boulevard Are Numbered." A short time later, the bar closed.

Buffy and the Breath of Life

One day, Bill and I went for a ride up in the hills around Redding. Usually, we would take our little toy poodle, Buffy, with us, but for some reason, we left him home that time.

When we got back to the house, we noticed right away that Buffy wasn't barking to greet us, as he usually would. Bill and I walked in and called for him. We found him lying on the floor near the sofa. I got to him first and saw that his eyes were fixed and glassy, and he wasn't breathing. He was stiff and cold. Bill and I both had been raised on ranches, and we had seen plenty of dead animals. We both knew our beloved little poodle was gone.

But we weren't ready to say goodbye yet. We started massaging his little body. I took his tiny muzzle in one hand and tried to revive him, blowing three short breaths into his mouth and nose. Bill and I prayed over him. I commanded death to leave and for life to come into him.

Almost instantly, Buffy stood up and shook himself, as if he had just awakened from a nap. He began to run around the house. As I watched my energetic, not-dead little dog running around and barking, I felt God say to me: "You will not only pray for dead animals but dead people."

A few weeks later, in the middle of a Sunday morning service, one of the deacons came into the auditorium. "There is a man out in the lobby having a heart attack," he said, and told all of us to start praying.

Bill and I were sitting near the doors, so, remembering what God's Spirit had said concerning issues of death, I got up and went into the lobby to see the man lying on one of the tables with a couple of people around him. To my surprise, no one was praying, so I prayed for him as I had prayed for Buffy, binding the spirit of death. The ushers had called 911, and it wasn't long until the ambulance came to rush the man to the hospital.

I walked with the paramedics to the ambulance, and when they had lifted the gurney into the vehicle, they suddenly turned to me. Before I could say anything, they put me into the ambulance, too! They must have assumed I was his wife. We were both transported to the hospital.

Meanwhile, back at the church, Bill was looking for me. The service was over, and everyone had left. Bill finally went out to the car, and as he drove away, he saw a woman up by the prayer house. Not knowing what else to do, he pulled over and asked her if she had seen me.

"I think she was put into the ambulance," the woman answered.

So Bill drove off to see if he could find me. He stopped at the first hospital, which was in downtown Redding, where he found me. I began to tell him the extremely funny story about the mix-up with the paramedics and how I was taken to the hospital with the patient. I was able to pray for the man the whole trip.

Everything happened very quickly, and I was just trying to be obedient to what God had told me after Buffy was raised from the dead. As Bill and I drove away, we left the outcome in the hands of the Lord.

To this day, it is in my heart to pray for people who have passed on and see them come back to life. I keep alert, looking for opportunities. It could happen! Because God cannot ever lie—it's all in His timing.

Faith Bigger Than a Bear

*B*ill and I liked to drive up to Whiskeytown Lake, which wasn't far from town, and relax at a place known as Carr Powerhouse. At the end of the lake, the powerhouse generates electricity through big flumes that brought in water from other lakes up in the mountains. The area has benches and pretty lawns and trees.

On that particular day when we arrived, we saw a pickup with a horse trailer. No one was around, but eventually, the owner rode up on a beautiful dark brown gelding. I started a conversation with her about the horse, and she told me that his lineage went back to one of the more famous racehorses of the time. I was impressed.

As she was leading her horse into the trailer, we suddenly had an uninvited guest: A bear was sprinting down the mountainside, right toward the road we were standing on.

Do you ever have those moments when you aren't afraid, even though your circumstances are pretty scary? That's what Jesus does for you. There wasn't a lick of fear inside me. On impulse, I started walking up the road—toward the bear. He was running fast, but I knew without doubt that God was in control and everything was going to be okay.

"Get in the car, Ma!" Bill said. "Get in the car, Ma!" It was a command and he said it to me several times.

But I wasn't paying attention to him. I kept walking toward the bear. I stretched out my hand and commanded loudly, "In the name of Jesus, GET OUT OF HERE!"

The bear turned and ran back up the mountain as fast as he could. In moments, he had disappeared.

As I returned to our car, I heard Bill and the woman talking. He later told me that she had asked, "Does she do this to bears all the time?" As if it might be an everyday occurrence!

"I don't think so," he calmly replied.

The Divine Bees

It had been a windy, rainy spring. One day, Bill's sister and brother-in-law, Becky and Bob, came to visit us from a city south of Redding known as Corning. Bob was a local pastor but they also were farmers. They had rented a ranch with prune trees, and used the crop for their income. The area is known nationwide for its almonds, dates, and prunes.

During our conversation, they said that their prune trees hadn't been pollinated because of the heavy rains. Their crop was at full blossom, but all the rain had kept the bees away. If you don't have bees to pollinate, there will be no crop.

As they got in their pickup to leave, I said, "Wait. Let's pray for your prune crop." So we prayed that God would give them a good crop and send in the bees. God can command blooms on a cut branch, and I knew He could bring in some tiny little helpers for our loved ones' prosperity.

Later, they called me up to tell me the agriculture inspector had come by to ask why they had such a large prune crop when other growers had none or next to none. Bob explained to the inspector that we had prayed for the bees, and the bees had come. God blessed them with a bountiful crop that year.

Ruth

*R*uth was an elderly woman with Alzheimer's who lived in our mobile park. She liked to go for walks, and I would see her walk past our home every day. I noticed she hadn't had a bath in a long time, so one day I went over to her house. I was appalled at what I saw when I walked in. She had gold-and-white carpet in her front room and had worn a black trail in it from walking back and forth from the pitted blacktop street into her house.

"Do you have anyone to take care of you?" I asked. "Do you have any children?"

"Yes," she said. "I have a daughter who lives in Chico, but she and her husband only come up during deer season."

I decided to start helping her because I could see that she wasn't able to help herself. For a while, I took her meals I had cooked, but then I began ordering meals from a service provider that would bring daily meals for her. Ruth said she didn't like to eat them because she thought they didn't taste good, so I would watch for the delivery vehicle and accept the meal for her. I'd bring it inside my house, put it on my own plate, warm it up, and take it to her. We would visit as she ate, and she would say, "This is really good!" She thought I had made it.

I also helped her with her bills and cleaning her home, but as time went on, taking care of Ruth began to be too difficult for me. I finally went down to the county human services agency and asked for someone to take over and assist in caring for her, because I was unable to continue.

A few days later, I looked out in the yard and saw Bill talking to a black man. I heard Bill say, "I don't know the answer to that question, but I think my wife will know, so come on into the house and we can ask her."

The county had sent this man to take care of Ruth. He was a nurse. I heard his British accent, and I asked where he was from.

"Kenya," he replied.

"Oh!" I said. "That's wonderful! Do you go to church anywhere?"

"Yes. I met some boys from a neighborhood church, and I go over there with them."

I asked if I could pray for him, and he agreed, so I prayed a blessing on him, and from that point on, the county took over Ruth's care. It wasn't long before they moved her into a convalescent home. I really loved Ruth. She had become a good friend. We couldn't get down to see her all that often because of my own physical condition, but one evening, I told Bill to go get the car. I knew we needed to see her.

When we arrived at the home, I sat beside her bed and talked to her, but there was no response. So I prayed for her instead. She was a Christian and had taught Sunday school to little kids for years. She and I had prayed together often. From my experience as a nurse's aide, I could tell by her vital signs that she was passing. Bill and I stayed with her as she went to be with the Lord. I was glad that we were able to be there for her last moments. Scripture says, "To be absent from the body is to be present with the Lord."

The Parting

*T*he Lord was so faithful to Bill and me throughout our lives. We had our ups and downs, as all people do, but I want to express my praise and thanksgiving to Jesus Christ, who led us through fifty-five years of marriage. We celebrated our fiftieth wedding anniversary on November 9, 2002.

One month later, on December 8, Bill was taking a nap on the living room floor, and I was sitting in a recliner nearby. I heard him mumbling in his sleep, but I didn't pay any attention.

The hour grew late, and I decided I'd better wake him because it hurt his back to sleep on the floor too long. When I went to wake him up, I discovered he had passed away. He had gone to be with Jesus. It felt as though my whole right side had been torn out—fifty-five years is a long time to share your life with someone.

For a few days, I pondered what Bill had been mumbling about in his sleep. I felt like the Lord told me that he had been talking to the angels who had come to take him home. Anyone who has lost a loved one immediately goes into mourning, but the Holy Spirit is the Comforter, and He was that during my time of mourning. I found Him to be my own faithful and true comfort.

Since Bill's passing, there have been some hard times, but I can tell anyone who reads this book that God is our faithful and loving heavenly Father. Life can be hard, but as the old song says, with Christ is my vessel, I can smile at the storms and go sailing on.

Life in Redding

*G*od has been good to me. I still live in the same mobile home Bill and I shared for years, and I'm active, doing my own yard work.

In these later years of my life, I unexpectedly find myself doing ministry down the street at a coffee shop. I ride my powered wheelchair down the hill to the shop, and after getting my coffee, I sit there and ask the Lord to open up a door for me so I can minister to the person He highlights to me. Every single time, He brings someone.

The shop tends to be busy, with students of different ages coming to study and spend time on the internet. Most of the people I meet are going through the three-year program at Bethel Church's School of Supernatural Ministry. They come from all over the world to attend this special equipping school.

Most of these students are asking questions about what the Lord wants them to do. Well, the only way to get the answer is by praying and seeking God. Very often, the students and I begin to build a relationship, and I invite them to my home. I think some of them are lonesome, and I fill a mother's or grandmother's role. It is exciting to hear the person you have been praying with say, "That is exactly what I have been praying about! Thank you."

I always tell them to thank God, because He's the One with the answers. I also like to say, "I'm just an old garden hose that the water of the Holy Spirit can flow through!" Cracks and all!

Looking back over my eighty-plus years of life, I have enjoyed the good times and have learned through the hard times that the Lord is faithful through it all. I know I have been royalty in His eyes all along. I am still marching on in Him, and He is writing the next chapter.

The End

CPSIA information can be obtained
at www.ICGtesting.com
Printed in the USA
LVHW031815090721
692281LV00004B/479